FAITHBU

Also available from Marshall Pickering
by the same author

JUNIOR YOUTH BUILDERS
BIG IDEAS FOR SMALL YOUTH GROUPS
with Nick Aiken

FAITHBUILDERS

Spiritual growth for youth groups
an action plan

Patrick Angier

Marshall Pickering
An Imprint of HarperCollinsPublishers

Marshall Pickering is an Imprint of
HarperCollins*Religious*
Part of HarperCollins*Publishers*
77–85 Fulham Palace Road, London W6 8JB

First published in Great Britain
in 1994 by Marshall Pickering

1 3 5 7 9 10 8 6 4 2

A catalogue record for this book is
available from the British Library

ISBN 0 551 02911-7

Typeset by Harper Phototypesetters Limited
Northampton, England
Printed and bound in Great Britain by
HarperCollinsManufacturing Glasgow

Contents

Contents

Acknowledgements

There are two people I would specially like to thank for their invaluable help in the writing of this book. The first is my wife, Beverley, for translating my scribbled pages into manuscript; the second is Imogen Grace, our baby daughter, who has been angelically good as we have put the finishing touches to the manuscript.

I would also like to thank Christine Smith for all her encouragement and suggestions as the book has taken shape, all the organizations that are included in the Radical Action section for being there, for always answering their phones in really helpful ways, and for letting me say nice things about their projects. Thank you, Tear Fund, Christian Aid, Care, Life, Christmas Cracker, Shaftesbury Society, and Baby Milk Action.

And finally, a big thank you to the members of Shalom, where the idea and practice of doing things 'a bit different' all started.

Preface

'We're fed up with being treated like kids.'

'This isn't school!'

'If only I was sure what I believed.'

'My friends would never come along in a million years.'

'We don't seem to be going anywhere . . .'

Working with young people has never been easy, but it seems to get progressively harder. As I travel around I find an unprecedented variety of styles of youth work available coupled with an immense diversity of young people with their unique situations, views and needs. The demand for an innovative and radical response to these needs has never been so great.

I often ask youth group leaders what their main aim is. The answer is almost always something like this:

'To see young people grow to maturity in Christ.'

'To help young people to follow Jesus.'

'To pass on the faith to the next generation.'

'To produce Christians ...'

Our different Church backgrounds and experiences often mean that we speak a variety of languages of faith, but our meanings, and our hopes for our young people, are one and the same.

For the young people we minister to this isn't so. They have a variety of languages and backgrounds and also come with different agendas and reasons for involvement in the groups we run. Some are there to chat, to be with friends or to make friends, as an alternative to the rougher secular club, or to grow in the Christian faith; they may come for many reasons or for none in particular. There are no simple answers to faithbuilding (just read a Gospel and see the problems Jesus had with the disciples!); we can only use our experiences, guidelines from others, ideas and suggestions and prayer. Faithbuilding is about 'growing' Christians; it's not about programme filling (even though it's full of programme ideas); it's about being REAL, RADICAL and RELEVANT; the three Rs of youth ministry.

Faithbuilding is the process by which we hope to see that transformation that causes a young person to move from just being a statistic in the numbers game (why do we get so obsessed with counting heads?) to growing as an active disciple for Jesus Christ.

Faithbuilding is not a quick fix and there are no short cuts. For too long we have hoped that merely by getting young people along to events, we would somehow turn them into Christians. The truth is that we have often sold young people short with an edited Gospel, pre-packaged and made easily digestible so that young people might swallow it, little realizing that its bland tastelessness was turning a generation away from God and into the arms of the cynics, activists and new-agers.

This book will explore what I believe are dynamic, Gospel-centred alternative goals for our work with young people:

Real relationships: Open and honest, empowering and participative, accountable, sacrificial and challenging.

Relevant teaching: Addressing the God-questions and real issues not just challenging personal ethics with a Christian gloss. Systematic, curricular, hitting real needs as well as the needs we think our young people have.

Radical action: Putting the Christian faith into action, showing that Christians really can make a difference, standing against injustice, oppression, poverty and all that stands in the way of the Kingdom.

In some small way. I hope this will contribute to our larger vision, so well expressed by Paul: 'It is him whom we proclaim, warning everyone and teaching everyone in all wisdom, so that we may present everyone mature in Christ. For this I toil and struggle with all the energy that he powerfully inspires within me' (Colossians 1:28–29 NRSV).

ONE

Faithbuilding Structures

There are many things that we, as youth leaders, can do very little about but that affect us greatly. We cannot influence how our young people respond to the group input, how much support they will get at home, what may happen at school, how much sleep they have had, or indeed any number of factors that will affect how they will respond to the programme.

The four things that we can influence most readily are:

1. Where we meet.
2. When we meet.
3. What we do when we meet.
4. How we treat our young people when we meet.

WHERE WE MEET

There may in fact be no options about where you meet: the church hall may well be the only place available. There may however be alternatives: we have used County Council Youth Work buildings for church youth work, and other youth groups have used Scout huts, British Legion headquarters, portacabins and buses(!).

The disadvantages of these other venues are usually the cost of renting the premises and the time taken to set up and take down. The advantages can be good: the premises are away from the church buildings and more accessible to young people from outside church circles. Also, if they are purposely youth work buildings we have found them adaptable and well resourced, which made the creation of a good youth work atmosphere easy. Whatever the building you meet in is like, there are a number of ways it can be adapted. 'Why?' you may ask. 'Why give more of your precious time to the arduous and often thankless task of setting up and laying out the room when you could be planning the session or praying, talking to your young people or taking extra time with your family?'

Of course, we must always be careful about maintaining a correct balance between all these things but spending a little extra time setting up your room to create the correct atmosphere or perhaps a different one to normal has clear advantages.

1. A space can be created where your young people can feel more at home and secure. This can lead to them being more open in discussions, more honest and more relaxed.

2. Setting up your room can encourage a clear group identity that is connected with the space, and this encourages your young people to feel they belong there. This is very useful if your hall is used for other things that the young people may attend at other times. It helps them to feel that this space and this time is uniquely theirs.

3. An inventive and creative room setting can also become something of a gimmick, something different enough for your young people to feel that they would like to bring their friends along to see and experience. It also helps them to bring people along if the place looks more friendly and carries less of the stigma of being a church building.

TEN WAYS IN WHICH TO 'SET UP' YOUR MEETING PLACE

1) Brainstorm ideas
When we first set up our Sunday evening group, THEOS (The Eight O'Clock Slot), we had imagined our room looking

something like a back alley: skyscrapers in the background, hall up-lights disguised as lamp posts, the stairs as a fire escape and dustbins for props. However, it ended up, very successfully, as a tropical island with palm trees and deck chairs, because the young people had a few different ideas from us.

One American youth group's room is decked out as and called 'Main Street'. Another group near us decided to give their room a more nightclub-like feel. They put in a false ceiling and lights and a bar in one corner. There are many ways in which it is possible to set up your meeting place: it is good to start with young people's ideas of how they would like it to be and how they can imagine it. You might be surprised at what they can come up with!

2) Lighting

The usual fluorescent strip lights often found in our church halls are very youth-unfriendly and school-like. So, what are the options?

1. Stage spot-lights. Use coloured gells (available from stage shops or local disco hire centres) and perhaps a dimming control board. The lights themselves are about £40 each and a dimmer board, if you have one made up for you, will cost less than £100. Four lights are enough for most places, and then all you will need is something to hang them from. Cost: £260. Good, but expensive!

2. Coloured up-lights (or down-lights). If you are allowed by your church council to fit more permanent lighting in your meeting place, then this can be achieved for about £60 (four up-lights, bulbs, switches and cables), providing you can find a friendly electrician to put them in for you free.

3. Home-produced lighting. Table lamps, car inspection lights, wall-mounted tracking with spot-lights, old standard lamps, etc can all be fitted with different coloured bulbs and

can give a room a real lift and a surprisingly different atmosphere.

Lighting serves a number of purposes. It can create moods (for instance, for a quiet period or for a noisy, more boisterous one). Lighting can also provide a focus. At our group we had programmed interview spots into our time together. The interviews took place on two old deck chairs. When interview time came around, the main lights went down and the orange light over the deck chairs came on. This led to some inventive suggestions and a banner or palm trees and a tropical island . . . and so it went on.

3) Furniture

Hard chairs and wooden floors are functional and practical but also not very pleasant or youth-friendly. Carpet makes a huge difference to young people's behaviour. This can be achieved even with a piece of carpet that is rolled out at the beginning and then put away at the end. Old sofas and chairs are easy to beg, as people are often looking for someone to take them away if they are buying a new one. Bean bags are great but expensive. Low coffee tables give a nice touch, but packing crates and painted or decorated boxes will do just as well. Create your room and your theme around the materials that are available.

The biggest problem with furniture, once you have it, is, of course, storage. Your group may love its cosy sofas at one end of the hall but to the Ladies' Fellowship Group or the Mums' and Toddlers' Group it may be a danger or an eyesore.

We were lucky enough to be given a supply of bar tables and stools when a local business reorganized itself. They looked really good but the only problem was that they were heavy and had to be stored in a small lean-to which stood up against the church. This meant that every Sunday they had to be lugged, dragged and carried to the hall and put away again after the youth group session.

The secret has to be active participation (on all levels!). This will not only save your back and your sanity, but will also increase the brain- and muscle-power available to solve the problem! Our solution was to stop meeting in the church hall and to meet in an unused county building instead. The tables and stools could be easily stored on the premises or even left in place, depending on what was on in the building between our meetings. Prior to this, however, lugging our tables and stools proved a quicker exercise if everyone helped; this also provided a chance for those who wanted to talk about something to stay back a little with a legitimate excuse!

4) Banners

'It's all in the banners,' one young person replied in answer to the question, 'What makes the group different?'

Banners can have a most striking visual effect on their own or especially when teamed with a different lighting effect or furniture. They can be hung from the ceiling or along the walls. They are great for covering windows to reduce the light on summer evenings or to improve the cosy feel of the meeting space in winter.

Banners can declare what the group stands for. They are fun and relatively easy to make. After our first attempt at painting them freehand, which was hard, time-consuming and difficult (and also resulted in low-quality banners!), we put the artwork on photocopy acetate and projected it onto the banner material. The shadow was easy to draw around in charcoal, pencil or tailor's chalk, and then we were able to paint it when it was laid flat with plastic sheeting underneath. The finished banners can be splattered with paint in contrasting colours over dry black lettering to add to the effect. This lifts dark colours and is especially effective when used with lighting.

As for the content of banners, we have used a variety of Clip Art, home-produced art work, computer graphics and lettering . . . in fact anything will do. The materials have ranged from wood to fabric from material shops or the market, depending on where we could get the best deal. This has not always been cheap, but with only a little expense, a bit of imagination and effort, and vast quantities of black emulsion paint they can look great.

5) Screens

In a large space, screening off an area in which to meet may be the only way to produce a more intimate, youth-friendly area. To buy new room dividers or display boards can be extremely expensive, but these things can be picked up quite cheaply when local companies refurbish their offices or move. Occasionally you may have the good fortune to discover some at a local Play Resource Centre or Scrounge Centre.

Home-made screens are fairly easy to construct, not as solid walls but as collapsible timber frames to which banners can be attached. These have the advantage of being not only cheaper but also highly individual!

Simpler screens may be made using the furniture itself . . . perhaps just the way in which the chairs are laid out. Furniture can be used to focus the group towards one corner of the room and away from the emptiness of the larger spaces and can be made really effective when combined with simple lighting effects.

6) Flooring

I remember vividly taking a group of young people away for a houseparty and, when ringing home, mentioning that all was going well and that the group were lying on their stomachs in a circle, heads in the middle highly engrossed in a spontaneous(!) Bible study. Hard, wooden floors make it very difficult for young people to get into what they consider to be comfy and relaxed positions. Carpets, rugs and off-cuts, all create softer spaces.

7) Audiovisuals

Not many youth leaders have the luxury of access to video projectors with state-of-the-art computer graphics on tap as well. For us, mere mortals, technical and audiovisual effects can be provided by almost anything, ranging from a cassette player in the corner (which is several decibels short of blasting anything, let alone a ghetto) to a TV and video alongside some public address system or music equipment. Often we have to make do with what we can scrounge or borrow.

Multiple TVs (if you can get hold of more than one for an evening) will run off one video. It might be nothing quite so grand as a video wall but you can put a TV in either corner of the room for a nice effect – and one that everyone can see!

Music Television (MTV) and modern music can be a great introduction to a Theme as well as providing something familiar for the newcomer, visitor or guest as background at the start. The responsibility for selection, recording and editing can be passed to one of the young people. We found that they can produce a really good selection that fits the theme of the meeting and upholds biblical principles.

8) Utilizing the layout of the room

How are we to use points 1 to 7 most effectively? This book aims at encouraging Relevant Teaching and Learning, Radical Action and Real Relationships. This involves shared responsibility – shared between leaders and members – participation, active learning, small groups, project work and many other types of activity.

Room layout can be a huge enabling factor in this style of youth work. Active participation and shared responsibility are important in its creation and the atmosphere it can create adds to many of the sessions and activities. For a programme which is fast moving and continually changing, a room with several different focal points can be a great benefit. For example:

notices can happen with everyone sitting on the carpet or bean bags facing the front; worship can happen with everyone turning around to face the band and a worship banner set up at the back of the room, and Bible study and small group work can happen on the carpet with everyone gathered in small groups.

How do you achieve this? The answer is, that as a youth leader, you don't. Constructing and then setting up a layout every weekend before the meeting is a nightmare (unless you are fortunate enough to have a room which you have exclusive use of all the time). The secret has to be in empowering your young people.

9) Empowering your young people

Young people can set up lights.

Young people can move furniture.

Young people can design, paint and put up banners.

Young people can move and assemble screens.

Young people can unroll and lay out carpet and rugs.

Young people can set up TVs, videos, music systems and
public address systems.

Young people know what a youth-friendly space is like.

Young people can be told what the programme contains
(but they also will know if they have been involved in
planning and are participating in its implementation).

Changing the nature of your meeting place involves young people taking some of the responsibility. As leader, you will need to give them that responsibility to deliver the goods but also to fail.

The starting point is, 'Who would like to help set up this meeting next Sunday?'

- work out the best time;
- find out if someone or a group of someones are willing regularly to take responsibility for organizing the setting up of the meeting place;

- give them the power to try out different arrangements and layouts.

With a large group of young people involved, it is easier for everyone: the tasks can be subdivided and everyone gets a say in how things are set up and laid out. For instance, you could have teams of young people, each team having its own area of responsibility:

Lay-out team: sets up banners, screen, moves furniture, etc.
Technicals team: deals with lights, TVs, music, PA, worship equipment, etc.

10) Other facilities

In addition to the up-front requirements of the space in which you meet, now is the time to think about what else you would like to do. For instance, do you need space for musicians? What about an overhead projector for words of songs or a projector for slides. Do you want a space for Holy Spirit ministry or a place for people to chat? What, if any, facilities do you want for food? Is there a tape library or book library, and if so where does this fit into the proceedings?

The only problem with all the extra equipment needed to create different atmospheres is the storage that is required if you do not have a room in which you can leave everything set up during the week or between meetings. Most church halls are multi-use buildings, and so rugs, banners, bean bags, lights and so on have to be stored somewhere safe between meetings. All too often, all of this stuff ends up in the youth leader's garage or, worse still, in his or her study! Sometimes, however, there will be space in the hall or church that can be used, negotiated or shared.

WHEN WE MEET

The traditional nights for meeting are Friday or Sunday. For some youth groups both Friday and Sunday are used. For others there are mid-week meetings or house groups. In fact, the range of times and possibilities is great. When we meet is not just dependent upon the times available but also on what we would like to do. This issue cannot be looked at in isolation. We need to be asking, 'What do we do when we meet?' and always balancing the time we give to our youth work against the time we give to our families and ourselves. It is crazy to be spending more time with other people's children than with our own.

WHAT WE DO WHEN WE MEET

This section is full of possibilities, ideas and potential models. They are not a blueprint for success. Every situation and every collection of relationships are different. Below are some ways in which youth groups work. They may be totally impossible in your situation: or it might be that they are *part* of the solution to some of the difficulties which you might have in a group at your church.

MODEL 1

It was eight o'clock: outside a couple of young people with long hair and leathers were finishing off their fags and getting ready to go in. Inside, the prayer time was over; the MTV was on and the coloured spot-light dimmed everywhere except on the banners. The bean bags, cushions and sofas were pushed back against the walls leaving enough space in the centre for slobbing out on the floor.

Young people opened the meeting. Someone prayed. Others reported on what was happening or had happened: a trip to climb three peaks, a flour tax campaign at a local supermarket (for every three bags of flour sold, the supermarket agreed to donate one bag to the youth group to send to Albania), details of mid-week house groups, a meeting for the Youth Service Planning Group and the obligatory request for material for the newsletter.

Some clips from *Beverly Hills 90210* and *Baywatch* appeared on the TVs, and the evening theme of 'Do you like yourself as much as God does?' was introduced. The group split up into groups according to where they felt they were at: 'Atheists Anonymous' went one way, 'Just Looking' another, 'Christian Basics' to a third room and 'Discipleship' stayed where they were. Some groups were led by sixteen-year-olds, others by those in their early twenties. The adult leaders gave input into Discipleship. As the groups came back together, there was sung worship, fag breaks for the desperate, cans of soft drink and coffee.

MODEL 2

It was a wet Friday so no one wanted to hang around outside. The lads were in first and headed straight for the pool table. The girls preferred to catch up on the latest and were clustered around one of the small tables. The room was pretty boring, except for a few round white tables, the pool table and a bar across one corner. The fluorescent lights were mostly off, and the room was lit by an assortment of lamps and things. After an hour the room was full of chatting, mixing teenagers. At first it was difficult to see who the members of the church group were, apart from the two who were serving behind the bar; but maybe they were the ones who knew the words to the *DC Talk* song coming out over the PA. Through the night, people came and went. The members behind the bar switched with the guys who had been listening to a talkative lad in the corner.

After throw-out time, the members gathered back to share about the evening, pray together and confirm the venue and time for the mid-week teaching and fellowship night.

MODEL 3

The laughter was infectious. The volume of voices spiralling upwards and the heaps of cut-up newspapers on the lounge floor became more and more chaotic. The group fitted well into Number 5's front room, but if it grew much bigger an extension would be needed! After the various groups had reported back on their activity, in came this mammoth heap of homemade cake (It was one of Mrs Grey's attractions – she sure knew how to cook!) and steaming mugs of hot chocolate.

As everyone munched, they divided up into groups of three, dug into their Bibles and got into the theme in more detail. Mrs Grey moved from group to group, lending a helping hand whenever anyone needed it. The session closed with quiet worship led by one of the young people and open prayer. Then it was time for planning, scheming and finishing the cakes . . . and see you at school, church, next time . . .

MODEL 4

The lads were there, waiting as Henry opened up. It didn't take long to put the chairs away, pull the screens and banners out of the cupboard, roll out the carpet, set up the lights and convert the hall ready for the evening. The evening session went with a real buzz. It was one of the top three from the topic survey from last term and so everyone had been looking forward to it.

The warm-up was followed by the main session, refreshments, a chance to pick up a tape or book from the library or a chance to talk or pray with one of the older young people or leaders. House groups that week were meeting and would be taking the whole theme further. A number of people wanted to know where the house groups were meeting and what happened there. A call came from the hatch: 'Grub up!' Tonight it was apple crumble and custard made by one of the young people. The members queued avidly for their 20p's worth. After the session, food was one of the passions of one member and had become a real hit. The menus ranged from crumble and custard to green jelly and ice cream, but all the food was popular.

Questions

The four situations above are based on real youth groups.

They help us formulate some questions that will help us look at our own structures.

1. What is the function of our main meeting? Is it:
(a) making contact with new people?
(b) evangelizing non-Christians?
(c) nurturing new Christians?
(d) disciplining committed Christians?
(e) preparing or equipping for action?

2. What balance should we have between catering for present members and reaching out to non-members? Should our aims include reaching out to different groups or sub-cultures of young people in our community?

3. Is it possible to disciple young people all together in one group?

4. Do we need opportunities to meet together in smaller units or in groups at similar stages in the Christian life?

5. How does the age make-up of the group affect the style and shape of what we are doing? How much of our programme should be youth led? And what should our responsibilities as leaders be: to do it ourselves or to train them to do it?

6. How do we balance group relationships, teaching and action?

Action Use the questions above as discussion starters for your leadership meetings or for your own reflection, thought and prayer.

In the four 'models' above, reference was made to a number of other activities outside the standard programme, some of which could be good to include in your youth work. Some of these ideas are included at the end of this chapter.

HOW WE TREAT OUR YOUNG PEOPLE WHEN WE MEET

I recently visited a 'successful' church to hear the youth minister talking about how they had grown to have over 400 young people attending their youth events, and how this number had declined to only a handful of bored and under-challenged young people.

The mistake they had made was to go down the 'entertainment road'. Bigger and better events eventually had failed to satisfy. Young people are not consumers of youth work. God's Kingdom is not like a marketplace where we offer a style of entertainment that some young people opt for while others opt for the nightclub, the football pitch or their home computers. We need to treat young people as partners, actively including them in our mission of building God's Kingdom.

The next chapter, Peer Ministry, explains at some length some of the ways in which we can do this in practice.

SPECIFIC ITEMS FOR THE MEETING PROGRAMME

Here are some ideas for the sorts of items that you might be able to incorporate into your meetings.

SERIOUSLY NAFF ADVERT AWARDS

Leaders and young people keep their videos on standby for that advert on TV which leaves them completely cold; the one which reminds you of nails across a school blackboard; the one which determines that you decide never to buy that product again . . . This is it. The opportunity to record it, show it and tell why you hate it.

On the night of youth group, members play the hated advert and in thirty seconds or less explain why its creators have done themselves less than justice. Have up to five entrants for the naffest advert and take a vote on it. Play the winning (or losing!) advert again at the end and save the video for the future in case the group misbehaves.

The thinking behind this session is to motivate and educate young people to look critically at the media, especially in the case of adverts, and to share some of their thoughts about this as well as their gut reactions.

Hint If you don't want to devote a whole session to this or don't have the time, why not get your young people to present one advert at the beginning of each session throughout the term. At the end of the term (or perhaps at a social over food) get them to vote.

COMMENT

This is an opportunity for your young people to talk about something which is important to them. Set up the framework for this so that there is a very relaxed atmosphere. Give the young people about three minutes to talk about something that is important to them. It could be a hobby, a memory, a hope for the future; something they feel passionately about, furious about or which concerns them. It doesn't matter *what* they talk *about* but it must be something *personal*. This is one of those things that you ask the group to do on a volunteer basis.

The idea for this came from some of our young people themselves. They had to run a session and they came up with this. It does have many benefits if your group is brave enough to take it on and do it properly. It brings to light areas for teaching in the programme, as the young people find they share the same concerns or confusions over issues, and it allows them to develop, in a safe environment, their powers of communication.

TESTIMONIES

Young people talking about how they came to faith is one of the most powerful ways in which they can witness to their non-Christian peers and also serves as a great encouragement to their Christian peers. Testimony says that God is alive and that he is active, that he is still doing the kind of things which he did in the times of the Bible but that he doesn't just act in the large matters but is concerned about small things in our lives.

Testimonies need to be 'non-religious' to be most effective: they need to be experiences told by young people in their own way and in their own language. Testimonies can all too quickly become churchified and cut off from young people's culture. Helping young people to express their faith in their own language and within their 'pre-Christian' culture is immensely hard, but it is essential if their witness is to be kept alive. Constantly having to reassess our progress in faith and to put it into our own natural language is an ongoing battle, but it keeps us from becoming stagnant. When asked how we are getting on in our faith, it is all too easy to use 'religious' terminology to reply . . . having to put our faith into our own words makes us think. It is such a shame that many young people change their expressions and faith stories when they tell their testimonies or indeed refuse to tell because they fear they are not good enough or worry because they don't phrase things correctly or don't fit into church life. A testimony given in a person's own words, no matter how rough, is a refreshing and stimulating experience and a necessary one in the witness to peers.

Testimonies also need to be *real*. They need to illustrate our struggles and not just the things that go well. They need to be given at the right time and at the right place.

REVUES

A youth group revue doesn't have to be the summer all-singing, all-dancing spectacular. It can take various forms, for instance, members reviewing books, tapes, videos, etc for the rest of the group. This can be done in several ways.

1. Ask a young person to review a book, tape or video. Lend them the item you have decided on. After a few weeks they share their views, criticisms and comments with the rest of the group.

2. The review is given an 'open floor'. The whole group is given the chance to comment on books in the library, the latest Christian book or tape, or perhaps a religious programme or issue which has been shown on TV. Members can share something they have found helpful or unhelpful, or an issue which has confused them.

3. If you have a youth group library ask the group who runs it to review books or tapes that have been added. Empower them with a budget to buy the books and tapes they feel appropriate.

The aim of this is to encourage your members to read Christian books and to listen to Christian music, and also to help them to share where they are in their faith in relation to a point of reference (i.e. a tape or book). It often makes faith issues easier to talk about if they are related to a book or tape, etc. You, as a youth leader, can also identify any significant issues or concerns that arise from these discussions and reviews and place them in the term's programme or discuss them with particular group members.

THINKING ABOUT ME

This is an opportunity for young people to take it in turns to talk about something that is important to them personally. The room, atmosphere and mood of this session need to be engineered so that everyone feels relaxed and unpressured. On a volunteer-only basis, the young people are given the chance to talk about something important to them. What they talk about can be anything, but it does have to be personal. This means that they can talk about a hobby, something they just like doing or something that concerns them. It must contain concerns and feelings and not statistics and figures. Encourage them to finish with why this particular thing is important to them.

The impetus for this activity came from some of our own young people. It has many benefits as it brings to light areas for teaching or house group meetings and allows the young people themselves to develop their communication skills and gifts for future use.

TWO

Peer Ministry

As youth leaders, we all experience the problems that peer pressure exerts on our young people: the young person who drifted away from club because it wasn't something which was *cool* with his friends; the young person who started drinking, smoking . . . we can all recognize the familiar picture.

Does peer pressure always have to be negative: is it possible for our young people to have a positive influence on their peers which will draw them towards the Kingdom? The answer to this has to be a resounding 'yes', but it will usually involve a cost for you as a youth leader – not in terms of money but in terms of power. Fostering successful peer ministry involves a handing over of power in real terms to our young people, and that hurts.

My first encounter with peer ministry was in open secular youth work. Some of the older young people who had been involved (those over eighteen) had been on a course which had raised their awareness of the issues surrounding AIDS. Enthused and equipped with information they came along to church youth group to discuss some of the issues involved. It was a really effective session. I had to admit that the group listened and learnt in a way which would not have happened if it had taken place in the usual way. OK, you might be saying to yourself, 'that might be fine in the case of some youth groups, but if you had seen *mine* on Sunday evening, you'd know they're not even responsible enough to make the coffee, let alone plan a programme or lead a session! Last time I asked them for ideas for the programme all I got in response was Ten Pin Bowling (again), Lazer Quest and a pub crawl.' But, hold tight and don't panic . . . this group of yours is ideal for transformation!

Empowering young people for peer ministry means giving *them* the power: they have the opportunity to do things, get them wrong and to fail and they have this opportunity not in the future but *now*. Alongside the possibility of failure they also have the potential for success. Young people are in the midst of the transition from childhood to adulthood in a society which has few rites of passage left. When do you become grown up? When you smoke, drink, drive or when you get married, get a job or leave home? For many young people who are yearning to be adult, the church only adds to their feelings of being cut off from adulthood.

We had our annual parish meeting recently. There were no young people present from the youth group despite the fact that lots take a full and active part in many areas of church life. I asked myself, 'Why?' Our church structures and attitudes keep our young people in childhood. It is just too risky to treat them otherwise and give them bits of power.

It is not only our churches that keep our young people in childhood: parents often do it. Youth leaders are viewed by some as people who are there purely to 'entertain' their offspring and keep them on the rails. Church youth work has become the nice alternative to the rougher secular youth work institutions and clubs. Once again, we as leaders are being pushed towards a no win situation. 'We give them what they want – entertainment – and they give us what we want – attendance at our events.' This is a long way removed from preparing our young people for a life of active and radical discipleship, self-sacrifice, following Jesus through thick and thin, good or bad. But this mentality, however small an influence, always seems to creep into our work with teenagers.

What does all this mean for us as leaders? We may well assent theoretically to all we have just read, but how in concrete terms can we go about instigating and preparing for this hand-over of power? And exactly how much power are we expected to hand over? It can be a tough concept to contemplate, especially when it takes all our time and energy to keep what we have going without taking on any more.

Peer ministry by definition cannot be *imposed*. The young people themselves have to own it. It has to be something that they are involved in and something that they go for wholly and with commitment. They have to be part of the process and not merely be recipients of your suggestion. We have to draw out and be aware of their concerns and anxieties in the face of something new. As with the introduction of any change, the concerns, anxieties and criticism will be greater about the new than about what has gone before (especially if you were not involved in the old!).

GETTING STARTED

A good starting point is to enable the young person to reflect on the present style of going about things. Talk about and share how they feel about it. Start with the facts and basics – time, place and topics – and move on to agendas, feelings and relationships. Try to steer this reflection away from the negative, and perhaps draw up a Group Analysis Questionnaire like the one at the end of this section.

STAGE 1: INFORMATION

Distribute the questionnaire to be completed. Say that the issues will be discussed the following week and that it would be helpful if group members could think about some of these things during the week so that everyone can participate in the discussion.

STAGE 2: CONSULTATION

From the analysis, you should be able to get a good idea of how members feel about the issues you suggested. It may be worth photocopying the questionnaire onto A3 paper and then filling in the most common answers compiled from all the replies so you can assess the group's feeling at a glance. Also fill in the five most popular youth group activities.

At the next meeting, talk about the replies. How do the young people feel about all the results put together? Were they surprised at any of them? What might the replies tell us about our group? What are our biggest strengths and weaknesses? (It is important to make sure that the answers in the discussion constantly bear in mind the group opinion as foretold by the questionnaires and not just the opinions of the most vocal.) Who has led the top five activities? Who could lead them? Why don't they?

STAGE 3: IMPLEMENTATION

There is a school of thought that suggests that changes should all be carried out at the same time. However, *process* is integral to youth work. Changes can be made gradually; involve everyone and take only one step at a time. This is important, even if everything seems too slow for some, as it will inevitably feel too fast for others. When Jesus sent the disciples on their first faith-sharing mission to the next village, they had already seen Jesus do what he now expected them to do. They had watched, asked questions and had a go with him watching what went on. Even after this preparation, he sent them off in pairs. As youth leaders, when we empower our young people, we need to involve them totally in the process.

There are several different ways to implement greater peer leadership within your group. No group can be totally peer-led in the same way that no group can be totally leader-dominated. In view of this, we are always involved in the process of gradually giving our young people more responsibility and leadership and of taking less on ourselves.

It is important, before we go any further to stress again that this is not an easy option. Enabling your kids to do more does not necessarily mean that you do less. Your role will change, but there is a real cost to you as a youth leader in the process.

As you pass on responsibility for things, the project that is being worked on will cease to be 'yours'. It may happen all in a rush or it may catch you unawares. It ceases to be 'yours' in order to become 'theirs'. This is fine if all the young people are doing initially is making coffee after the evening service, but it can be amazingly painful to see your 'baby' become someone else's. This happens and is at its most hurtful (and yet its best) when projects go well. What if the project happens to be 'the alternative worship', 'the annual breakfast' or 'preaching at the youth service'? How will you feel when they take the responsibility for the ministry and don't want you to do anything? Our heads often tell us that this is right: we're developing leadership skills and helping the group to grow; but our hearts might feel a whole range of emotions: 'I do all the hard work and they're doing the things that I like doing. Do they really need me?'

We recently set up a group to run our alternative worship and to plan multimedia events. We had already had three trial runs of these events with me at the organizational helm, and it was time for the young people to start taking some of the responsibility. Four young people plus two students from the university who were part of the band providing the music made up the new planning group. Our adult leaders were not present at the meeting but the young people reported back all that they had planned at the end of the meeting. Great! All we had to do in the proceedings was to book the church . . . the young people were to do everything else! The following day, one of our young people called round. He had to do a three-minute talk and wanted to ask, 'How do I do a talk?' So instead of choosing videos or songs for the alternative worship, I was to spend my time explaining how to give a talk. It has to be for the benefit of our youth work and the Kingdom of God that we encouraged our young people to lead! And won't it be great if they can do it better than us?

GROUP ANALYSIS QUESTIONNAIRE

NAME:

On the following:

score 1 if you strongly agree with the statement
score 2 if you mostly agree
score 3 if you neither agree nor disagree
score 4 if you mostly disagree
score 5 if you strongly disagree

BELONGING

1. This Group is a place where I feel safe   1   2   3   4   5
2. This Group is a place where I feel I have been listened to   1   2   3   4   5
3. I have close friends in this Group   1   2   3   4   5
4. New people are welcome here   1   2   3   4   5
5. I sometimes feel left out in this Group   1   2   3   4   5

PARTICIPATION

1. The Youth Group holds a high priority for me   1   2   3   4   5
2. I feel needed at Youth Group   1   2   3   4   5
3. I would like to be more involved   1   2   3   4   5
4. I sometimes feel like a spectator at Youth Group   1   2   3   4   5

List the top five activities which you feel we do as a group

	Who leads?	Who could lead?	Could I lead?
1.			
2.			
3.			
4.			
5.			

CONTENT

1. The topics we look at at Youth Group are boring		1 2 3 4 5
2. The topics we look at are important		1 2 3 4 5
3. The topics we look at are important to me		1 2 3 4 5
4. The topics we look at are important to others		1 2 3 4 5
5. There are more important things to teach on		1 2 3 4 5

GIFTS

Below is a list of gifts, abilities and talents. Put a ring around any that you feel that you might have and put a cross through any that you feel other members of the group have.

Listening, singing, acting, reading, washing up, praying aloud, playing an instrument, drawing, painting, cooking, carrying chairs, climbing ladders, using PA, electrical skills, using lighting, writing songs, drama, dance, photocopying, typing, administration, speaking to other people, shopping, cleaning up, helping others, organization, sense of humour, sewing, giving good advice, fun to be with.

EMPOWERING YOUR YOUNG PEOPLE

Empowering young people for peer ministry can be done in many ways and it is important that you find a way which is appropriate to your group.

THE YOUTH COMMITTEE

These have a number of advantages:

1. Youth committees enable you as a leader to get to know a small group of members well. Always show an interest in their lives outside the group and leave time, perhaps over coffee, to talk about other things as well as the topics of the meeting.

2. A suggestion may be to hold some or all of the committee meetings at committee members' houses. As you are meeting on their turf, they will feel more relaxed and you will also get the chance to meet some of the parents informally (or at least get to know what they look like!).

3. Through the committee the young people in the group can share the responsibility for different areas of the programme. They can express their views through their representatives. Committee members can be given their own special areas of responsibility, e.g.

Secretary: writes letters, receives post, keeps committee
 meeting minutes . . .
Treasurer: collects subs, buys biscuits, keeps accounts . . .
Publicity: produces posters, keeps notice board up to date . . .
Social secretary: arranges the group's social events . . .
Sports representative: arranges the group's sporting events,
 fixtures, training . . .
Prayer secretary: produces prayer diary, opening-in-prayer
 rota . . .

The positions you have on your committee should be tailor-made for your group. These could include anything: Tuck Shop Manager, Social Action Organizer, Overseas/Missionary Representative . . . the list can be endless.

4. The committee is a good forum for ideas to be discussed, prayed about; problems and anxieties can be shared and group problems brought out into the open. It should be a place where members can feel at home and relaxed and also one where they can be honest, not feeling intimidated either by leaders or by factions within the youth group as a whole.

5. Establishing a committee enables you to give recognition to faithful and committed established members of the group and yet also to build up self-conscious and shy members.

6. The increased contact between leaders and committee members gives more opportunities for one-to-one discipleship. Members will see how we relate to God in everyday life. They learn about God as they see him active in our lives and, we hope, they will begin to see him more in their own lives.

Potential problems

It all sounds great, doesn't it?! If every members' committee which was formed was dynamic and active, then all would be rosy. Sadly, they often fail to live up to their full potential through lack of monitoring and continuous management. Some of the things which stop them fulfilling their potential are discussed now.

Committee-itis This is a nasty contagious disease, often passed on from infected church committees. It is a horrible, disabling plague which causes the group to become so wrapped up in agendas, minutes and matters arising that nothing is ever done.

Overburdened committee If the tasks that have been allocated to the committee are unachievable, they either do not get done at all or are done badly. This creates a very real sense of failure within the group and devalues the members, both as individuals and as the committee. An example of this might be that the Social Secretary is expected to organize a social event each week and have it advertised around all the local schools by the Publicity Rep. Tasks need to be appropriate and realistic.

Passenger-carrying committee Both newly created and established committees can create the situation where the youth group become like inactive passengers. The committee do all the work while the rest of the group feel that everything is the committee's responsibility so they don't offer to help and eventually lose interest. A balance needs to be maintained, as the youth group needs to feel *represented* by the committee and the committee needs to feel *supported* by the rest of the group.

Clique-ridden committee Relationships can become so close within the committee that it becomes an exclusive cell within the greater group and unwelcoming to others. The rest of the group can feel left out, rejected and powerless.

Talkshop The committee can become a place where lots is said and great discussions take place, but nothing ever gets done. Everyone enjoys it but no one does anything. The group starts to wonder what the committee does.

Making the most of a youth committee

There are a number of ways in which we can capitalize on the positives of a youth committee and minimize the negatives.

Give real responsibility This includes the possibility of failure. Real responsibility doesn't mean that the young people think they have the responsibility when in reality they don't – a situation full of safety nets and hidden protections given by worried leaders, as sometimes happens. Real responsibility lays open the possibility for failure. If young people do not get this opportunity to fail they can never get anything wrong. If we, as leaders, give in to our anxieties and always step in to avert disaster, they will never learn . . . and neither will we!

Give wider responsibility All too often, members' committees deal with only the peripherals of youth ministry. We use it as a consultation group, to find out about how the wider group feels, and not as an action group. Often we don't have to look far for the reasons for this: what if we were to pass over the control of the entire programme – will all they do be 'relationships', food events and trips out?

There are several ways of avoiding this. One good way is for you and the members' committee to draw up a topic sheet like the one at the end of this section. The committee distributes the sheets to the group, who fill it in. The committee correlates the replies and then meets with the youth leaders to help incorporate the topics into the programme.

Programming is only one area in which the committee can have a share of the responsibility. Every aspect of our youth work can be gradually drawn into their range of responsibility as they grow in ability and confidence.

Give active responsibility The objective of Peer Ministry is to encourage young people towards an active faith. Inseparable from responsibility is action. Responsibilities need to involve an element of 'doing'. As well as being a record of what was said, committee meeting minutes should include a list of actions stating what is to be done and who is to be responsible for doing it. This also has the advantage of bringing discussions, plans and conversations down to earth. It is one thing to suggest something if it is the youth leader who will have to carry it out; it is quite another to suggest it if you are going to have to do it yourself!

Take collective responsibility Don't leave your young people isolated or alone. If something does go wrong, committee members learn from the mistake and accept their part in it, rather than one particular individual being left to carry the can. As leader, you need also to be looking after each individual concerned. It can be good, especially with younger

THE TOPIC SURVEY

✓ two topics from each section.   * your three top choices.

IN MY LIFE

___ Being radical
___ Leisure time
___ Dealing with zits (and the like)
___ Coping with parents
___ Self-worth (Oh, bummer ...)
___ Depression (No, thanks!)

___ School/college
___ My Family (and other animals)
___ Peer Pressure (It's heavy, man!)
___ Stress (Can you take the pace?)
___ Temper (Agggrrrhhh!)
___ Temptation (I didn't want to but ...)
___ How to balance life (and not fall off)

HAPPENING ROUND ABOUT

___ Sex
___ Doing the drugs game
___ Music (Is it evil????)
___ Racism
___ Does your tongue flap (in the breeze)
___ Loneliness (You're not the only one)

MY CHRISTIAN LIFE

___ Sharing my faith? (I just couldn't)
___ Time/talents/dosh
___ Perseverance (when the going gets ...)
___ Dealing with Satan
___ Fasting
___ Staying awake (while reading the Bible and not
     snoring in prayer)
___ Fruit of the Spirit
___ Doubt (that nagging feeling)
___ Faith (fact or fiction)
___ Sin (sounds good but makes you puke)
___ Discipline
___ Getting God's handle
___ Getting muscles for God

AT CHURCH

___ Church
___ Worship (more than a gooey feeling)
___ Spiritual gifts (toys or triumph)
___ Spiritual warfare
___ I want to serve God (but how?)
___ Authority

___ Relationships
___ Food (yummmmmmy)
___ Materialism (3 reasons why you could have
    a Porsche)
___ Prejudice
___ Love
___ Drinking

OUT IN THE WORLD
___ Abortion
___ Death and dying
___ Euthanasia
___ Divorce
___ Pacifism vs War
___ Suffering
___ Starvation
___ Why the poor countries stay poor (Give the
    lil' guys a chance)
___ Drugs
___ Homosexuality
___ Environment
___ Money

___ Servanthood (without being a doormat)
___ Prophecy (speaking God's words)
___ Denominations (Why are there so many and
    who's right?)
___ Easter
___ Christmas
___ Pentecost

GROWING IN KNOWING
___ Holy Spirit
___ The Twelve (Jesus' big bodge?)
___ Christian business
___ Lost in the New Testament
___ Lost in the Old testament
___ Other religions
___ God's promises
___ Creation/evolution (Were all the dinosaurs
    wrong????)
___ Who's who: Bible
___ Jesus' life
___ Who killed Jesus Christ?
___ Heaven and hell

groups, to allocate each member to a leader who will act as 'guardian angel'. The leader will check how his or her 'charges' are doing and help them out, support them or encourage them as necessary.

ACTION GROUPS

This is a much less formal method of peer ministry than the youth committee, but it can nevertheless be very effective. These groups are small, task-orientated and member-led, and each group has a specific purpose. They have proved a successful way of motivating and mobilizing young people. These small groups can take many forms:

Music Group provides worship at services, meetings and events.

Drama Group provides (and usually writes) sketches and drama for services, meetings, street work, etc.

Road Crew moves equipment to events, and moves furniture for services and special props for drama, dance, etc.

Dance Group provides dance for services, meetings, street work, workshops, etc.

Room Set-Up Group lays out furniture, banners, props and scenery for drama.

Lighting Crew plans and then sets up lighting for alternative worship, performances, dance, etc.

PA Team arranges the sound system for music.

Prayer Posse organizes prayer cover and intercession rotas, prayer ministry at events and meetings.

Banner Group designs, plans and paints banners, backdrops or even rooms for meetings in liaison with other groups.

Third Track Team responsible for education and raising awareness on Third World issues. Runs sessions on these topics using Tear Fund Third Track and similar material.

House Groups can be youth-led groups for Bible study, fellowship and prayer.

Video Reporting Team reports what's on, what's happened, records news clips at events, outings, meetings etc. These can be used for advertising for campaigns and fund-raising, surveys, etc.

Video and Music Tapes Group prepares taped music and linked video film in conjunction with the Video Reporting Team for multimedia and alternative worship events.

Social Action Team plans Social Action events and campaigns. They can be responsible for doing the research on concerns and motivating and mobilizing the response. They must also keep the youth group informed of progress on issues of concern and projects supported. They can link with Prayer Posse for intercession and with the Publicity Group as necessary.

Publicity Group Organizes and prepares programme cards, posters, flyers for events, prayer calendars, educational leaflets for distribution and home-produced evangelistic leaflets in conjunction with all the relevant groups. They can arrange for press cover at any events where this is needed. They are also responsible for compiling contributions for either a youth newsletter or magazine or for the Parish magazine.

Planning Groups plan any events that come up and allocate tasks to any other groups. They should keep everyone informed of what is going on.

Any of these groups can, of course, be established at any time and for quite a deliberate purpose, e.g. for a special event. You may find that once one kind of group is established, then many others spring up seemingly from nowhere. If you start with a planning group, perhaps for an alternative worship event or youth service, you may find that music, dance, drama and technical-based groups appear from that quite naturally.

Our plethora of youth-led action groups began with our Worship Band. We had a team of committed young musicians who visited other churches and youth groups to lead worship. Other young people who were not musicians expressed a need to do something to put their faith into action and also to complement the ministry of the Worship Band. From this came a Technical Support Group, a Dance Group, a Lighting Crew . . . all of a sudden we discovered a real heart for mission among our young people. We had groups learning circus skills, groups discovering and experimenting with alternative forms of worship and generally being creative with their faith. Sometimes it took a little input from a leader to get things going, as with the drama group writing their own material, at other times it just happened by itself.

The next steps

There are six ways in which you can help this process to happen.

Step 1: Identify your members' gifts. It may be that God wants your young people to be active in entirely different ways from those which have already been mentioned. The scope for areas of action will be to some extent determined by the specific gifts and talents of your group.

Step 2: Prayer. The ministries that God is calling your group to be involved in will be found by seeking his will. Is he calling you to be involved in social action within the local community, fund-raising for mission, Third World campaigns . . .? The list goes on and on, and there are so many opportunities; it's good to seek guidance.

Step 3: Offer the young people the chance to get involved. This may be through national events as *Christmas Cracker* or *It's Life Jim*, or through local initiatives, or through a specific suggestion of a group member.

Step 4: Meet with the young people. Encourage, support and pray with those who want to get involved.

Step 5: Let them get on with it. Do not do the work for them. Perhaps don't be at every meeting they have; be a facilitator rather than a dictator!

Step 6: Praise them. Give them encouragement, tell them they have done well, try to find positive things to emphasize even when they have made a mess of it. Give them the limelight if the project works and if it doesn't then evaluate it together and start again.

Some of your young people will inevitably be involved in more than one group, and there is always also someone who wants to be involved in everything! It is a good idea to monitor the number of 'meetings' that this may generate for your young people. Perhaps limit the number of activities and events and responsibilities they have each week, especially around exam time. Action groups usually meet on an 'as needs' basis, so they may not need to meet every week.

The groups themselves carry responsibility for their area. If they don't do what they are meant to, then there should not be a leader who will run around covering up for them: part of the delegation of authority involves taking the risk that what you have left them to do might not appear. You will probably find that as time goes on, natural leaders will emerge from each group. This will make keeping a tab on things a bit easier as the leader will be a little more reliable than some of the others and will motivate the members of each group into getting things moving.

Action groups are one way of beginning to solve the problem of committee-itis as outlined above by helping young people to realize that Christianity is more than just 'saying' the right things, but about 'doing' and 'being'. Also, as one of the best forms of active participation for groups, action groups allow much more to get done. They give young people a first-hand experience of Christian ministry, and they help potential Christian leaders to be identified and help train a new generation of experienced and creative leaders for the future.

THREE

Real Relationships

'I can only be that which I am willing to share with you'
(John Powell)

INTRODUCTION

For today's teenagers this does not leave much opportunity to be at all. Family breakdown is at an all time high, the pressures of work mean increased demands on family time, the amount of meaningful interaction between teenagers and their parents is minimal: meals are often self-service affairs and conversation between young people and their parents (especially with their fathers) is reduced to virtually nothing. The average father spends about fourteen minutes a week talking to his teenager, and eleven of those minutes are usually negative.

The evidence for this apparent lack of 'relationship' in the world of today's teen can be seen on any Friday evening, in any inner city, town or suburb: disaffected youths hanging out, their parents unperturbed by and uninterested in their whereabouts. It is demonstrated in the rising crime figures and most especially in the teenage suicide statistics. Young people who are overtaken by hopelessness, despair and a meaningless life are opting out.

If the situation at home is unpromising and 'unsuitable' for any kind of relationships, what about the peer group? At first sight the lack of relationships in the family seems to have been filled by numerous, multifaceted relationships with peers. Friends seem to provide some kind of identity and a sense of belonging. But, if we take a closer look, we see that this is really ceasing to be the case. Young people are still lonely, frightened of being rejected and despairing so much that they are being forced to do things that they do not want to do and do not even like doing in order to find the slightest relief from loneliness.

WHAT MARKS OUT A REAL RELATIONSHIP?

Real relationships are marked by characteristics different to those we see riddled through our society.

UNCONDITIONAL LOVE

As youth leaders, we accept young people unconditionally: they are valuable and special. They may never become Christians but we love them just the same. This love is not unsubstantial and superficial. It means that we make people welcome. It means that we take an interest. It means we look after other people's needs before our own. It means that the youth group does not divide down continuously into cliques, leaving people out. Unconditional love is not just something that the leader does; it is something that is inherent in the group because God is there.

COMMUNITY

Our young people belong to a *group*. We do things *together*. The group is marked by being more than a collection of individuals. The Bible talks about the Church as a body and so it really should be with our youth groups; they are also the body of Christ. As we, as leaders, share in the troubles, hassles and anxieties of everyone else in the group, as we suffer together, have fun together, celebrate and work together the group slowly becomes community.

This all sounds rather like an ideal situation, especially if we cast our mind's eye back to last Sunday evening and remember that half the group refused to talk to the other half; so and so still will not come because she feels left out and Adam still dominates the group with his views! Community is not something that just appears; it has to be striven for, worked for and built up gradually. The more things that we do together and struggle through together the more a community is established.

MEANING

If life really is meaningless, so are relationships. People, as a necessary consequence of a meaningless life have to be disposable. The quest is always for the 'buzz', the high; that moment that helps us forget our nothingness. Relationships are just one more analgesic, along with drink, drugs, music, activity and sex. They are the things that make existence bearable.

It is essential for Real Relationships that we demonstrate that there is meaning to life and that this meaning permeates everything that we are and backs up and spurs on everything that we do. Life does have a meaning: there is a God who is concerned for every hair of your head, every second of your life and for your future in eternity. The fact that life does have a meaning affects how we treat the old, the young, people with disabilities or people from different ethnic origins. Real Relationships transcend culture, class and other barriers.

LISTENING

No one seems to have any time these days. Everyone is too busy or too concerned with getting their own say in what is going on to hear what other people are saying. Our youth groups need to be places where young people are listened to. This might mean looking at our structures and patterns so that the young people themselves are the most important things on our agenda. It is in listening to each other and sharing honestly that relationships develop.

There is a quality of relationships that is apparent if we listen to each other and share honestly; this is different from the way people are treated by the world. Young people are crying out for the honesty and empathy that this kind of relationship contains and if our group is one with these kinds of relationships in it, young people will be drawn in as they are challenged to ask, 'Why are these people different?'

SPIRITUAL GROWTH

The presence of the Holy Spirit is the foundation for Real Relationships. Without God's active transformation of our lives, without the experience of his forgiveness and love, without the example of Jesus and the power of the Holy Spirit, our relationships will fall pitifully short of God's standards and possibilities.

ENCOURAGEMENT

Our groups should be places where we encourage people to grow spiritually, not just by the things which we say but by all that we do. Looking back on my life, it is those people who have encouraged me who have made the most impact.

Real Relationships are ones where we help each other to press on towards the goal. Real Relationships are ones where we do not need to put others down to build ourselves up; rather, they are ones in which we are built up ourselves by building others up.

Translating this into a youth group isn't quick or easy. As it happens, however, the group will become a place that is attractive to newcomers and challenging to members: a group in which Christianity is not just something we talk about but in which it is evidenced in the reality and clarity of our relationships with one another.

DEVELOPING THESE REAL RELATIONSHIPS

These relationships need to develop in a number of different dimensions:

1. Upwards The most important relationship in the picture is our relationship with God. Every other relationship, no matter how special, is transient. This one is eternal. How to develop, strengthen and maintain this relationship is crucial.

2. Inwards The relationships within the group. How to be honest with each other, how to support and care for one another, how to listen, identify gifts, cope with disagreements, what to do when new people join and all the problems of being a group.

3. Outwards The relationships with other people, with young people who are not part of the group, with adults and parents, with children and grandparents: how do we relate to the variety of people that make up the world beyond the group?

4. Downwards The relationship within oneself. Identifying the inner struggles and problems. Recognizing strengths and weaknesses. Discovering how God is changing, challenging and transforming your inner self.

Real Relationships are a product of Radical Action (see chapter 5) and Relevant Teaching (see chapter 4). Here, in addition, are a number of ideas and sessions to further these kinds of relationships particularly.

UPWARD RELATIONSHIPS (WITH GOD)

Spiritual growth of the youth group is not very often the number one item on many youth leaders' list of priorities.

After 'What are we going to do on Sunday Night?' usually comes the 'how-many-did-we-have-last-night' paranoia of the following Monday. If we have good numbers and we are still finding new-ish things to do then we feel that we are doing OK, or at least that the pressure is off from the Church leadership.

Even if the number we have attending is important to us leaders, it doesn't mean that, if the group itself was asked the same question, it would feature on the group's priority list.

One of the fundamental tasks which we have is to establish firstly on our own lists and then, with more difficulty, on theirs, is that spiritual growth is important. The ways in which you can foster an atmosphere for spiritual growth and encourage your young people to have a desire to grow are many and varied. Often the way in which you will carry out any of the suggestions below will depend upon the size and type of group that you have. In the same way that you will find you have to adapt these ideas, you may also find that the results you get will differ. God created all young people as individuals and their spiritual growth will be as individual as they are.

Worship

In a sense, everything that we do is worship. We are constantly praying and working and worshipping in our youth programmes. Many youth groups begin with a time of singing Christian songs and most start or finish with a prayer of some kind. It is good, in addition to this, to make space for cultivating a sense of the awe and mystery of God. Teenagers experience noise and activity most of the time and so to experience such a complete contrast to this can be extremely valuable. There are plenty of ways in which this can be done, drawing upon a wealth of Christian tradition from across the whole spectrum.

Silent prayer Use a candle or cross as a focus.

Biblical meditation Reflect in quiet on a passage from Scripture or perhaps on a poem or the lyrics of a worship song. Be imaginative. Perhaps try reflection in quiet but also with movement or mime.

Quiet worship songs Instead of the latest praise songs, use reflective, quieter songs to begin the evening.

Music Both modern and classical music have great power to touch the senses and sometimes to help us to think, pray, or just to sit in front of God.

Water 'He who comes to me will never be hungry; he who believes in me will never be thirsty' (John 6:35). Pass around a cup of water in silence using it as a focus for meditation on the above sentence from John's Gospel. Or take your group to a mountain top, high hill or park . . . what can they experience, smell, taste, see and touch? Read together Psalm 8 or a section of Psalm 104.

Awe and mystery are not things that we can necessarily *create* but by creating the space and the opportunity for these things they become experiences that are possible. We have found that small groups are often best for the more reflective exercises, although with a mixed group of Christian and non-Christian young people, we have had over 25 participate successfully.

We can also worship God using movement instead of voice. This is especially good in smaller groups and in larger ones where no one is confident about using their voice. One of the best ways of using movement is by utilizing sign language. Either invite a deaf person (perhaps a deaf chaplain) into the group for the evening or make up your own more pictorial actions to a verse, song or Bible passage.

Spiritual journals

When I was a young person I kept a diary. After becoming a Christian this habit sort of became 'Christianized' and it was transformed into a kind of journal. It was a record of what was happening in my spiritual life, the people I was praying for, what God was saying or doing . . . whatever I was experiencing or feeling. Looking back, this helped me to see how God had answered prayers in a longer term perspective than my memory alone would have allowed.

Spiritual journals and prayer diaries are more familiar in some denominations than others but they are a valuable resource for some young people. Some find them helpful and a liberating experience; others find that it is just too much hassle to keep them.

At its simplest, a journal is a notebook for writing down prayers and thoughts from Bible study. At the other end of the spectrum there are books and journals specifically engineered to help Bible-based thoughts or individual prayers.

One-to-one discipleship

The Christian life is hard work when you are trying by yourself. More and more young people in our youth groups today are coming from non-Christian homes where they lack the support and nurture for their faith which they might get in a Christian family. One-to-one discipleship is a way of pairing up your young people to disciple one another and support one another.

Each new Christian or 'younger' Christian to come into the group is paired with a more experienced Christian of the same sex. There is no need to panic if you look around your group on a Sunday evening after reading this and can't seem to find many of what you consider to be 'experienced' older Christians. The exercise can work with any level of group. The important thing is that everyone is paired with someone they are compatible with and feel comfortable with. Two new Christians in a pair can share their difficulties and joys and discover answers to problems together. The pairs make a commitment to help each other grow spiritually by:

1. Praying together and for each other.
2. Reading the Bible together.
3. Sharing each other's burdens and problems.

Pairs can meet as often as they want and wherever they want. You may find that some want to meet at school, some may meet less regularly but talk on the telephone a couple of times a week.

Some advantages to the youth group of one-to-one discipleship are:

• New Christians are helped with the disciplines of prayer and Bible Study as they learn 'on the job';

- Problems may be picked up earlier than they would normally have been; this especially refers to those who are new to the group and who have little or no Christian experience;
- The young people will begin to develop pastoral and leadership skills, which gives them confidence when asked to lead a house group or when they have to talk to their friends or lead someone to Christ;
- The whole process releases leaders' time, enabling you to be more *proactive* rather than totally *reactive*: initiating and evaluating rather than responding to just what happens moment by moment.

Learning together to minister

There are times in our Christian lives when we all feel totally devoid of any strength and power. Our young people, like us, can feel this and learn this in many different ways. It may be wrestling with something that they know is sinful but can't quit doing; it may be feeling totally bewildered in bereavement or after splitting up with a boyfriend or girlfriend; it may be suddenly feeling that they have not got all the answers to life's problems; it may be confusion after meeting another Christian or going to another meeting where our young people sense that there was something different.

In our Christian lives, the Holy Spirit is our power line. He shows us Jesus, He helps us to understand Scripture and gently nudges our conscience when we do wrong. Whatever our churchmanship, we have all had these experiences when God felt especially near. Part of building up spiritual community in our churches and youth groups is being honest enough to share our problems, sins and difficulties and to minister to each other.

We can minister in so many ways. We can be there for each other and pray for one another, asking God to strengthen and encourage . . . When ministering there can come a point when we don't know what to pray for or how best to help. These times can be the best times for introducing young people to the gifts of the Holy Spirit in their prayer for each other. Bible studies on Acts and 1 Corinthians can help explain tongues, intercessory prayer, words of knowledge, and there are plenty of books on the market that cover these issues.

I wandered to the back of the church as the worship band led the congregation in quiet worship. A thousand spots of light from the mirrorball slowly moved around the walls to show visibly that this was the quiet and reflective time of our alternative worship.

Looking around, I could see the teenagers from the Prayer Posse praying with those who had responded to the talk or just listening or comforting those who were in tears.

Our Vicar was standing quietly at the back and it ran through my mind that I must thank him for coming out to support us in prayer . . . it was then that he came up and asked if anyone was going to pray with him. Catching the eye of two of the Posse I left them to gently minister to him.

Here were young people ministering in the power of the Holy Spirit to a Vicar; God's way of showing how upside down his Kingdom is.

Holy Spirit ministry is, in a nutshell, our young people being open to and using the gifts of the Spirit, giving God a chance to dictate our spiritual growth and asking him to come into our lives rather than filling our prayers just with words.

INWARD RELATIONSHIPS: WITH EACH OTHER

Youth groups can sometimes feel as if they are more akin to a bunch of pool balls on a pool table than a fully functioning group: all tightly bunched one second and scattered all over the place the next. The role of the youth leader comes somewhere between being the cue and the white ball: trying to get them all into the right pockets and then back together. It seems things never stay still long enough. Just as soon as one person has fallen out with someone else, they have already made up with another, no matter what the age!

How can we develop a sense of community on such an unstable surface? It feels as impossible as potting the pool balls on a moving pool table. It isn't easy, but we need to try to foster community, develop the trust, honesty and love that will cope with difficult people and people who are different and allow them to be included and welcomed into the group. Relationships that we have built, teaching and the indwelling work of the Holy Spirit help to effect change, but sometimes circumstances may force us to act *more directly*. The unresponsive clique within the group or the continually left-out individual means that we have to act to force change to happen.

Are there ways in which we, as youth leaders, can help the relationships within our groups to stay good and positive? How should we handle some of those sticky situations that inevitably arise because they aren't always good and positive? Below are some important ways to achieve our goal.

Have good communication systems Ensuring that there are good channels of communication between leaders and young people means that grievances can be aired freely as they happen, misunderstandings can be sorted out and soothing oil can be poured on situations before they get worse. Likewise, good communication among the leaders and a common understanding of the group's aims and purposes are vital.

Don't be afraid to address the issue directly If there is a clique, split it up. Make sure that the clique members are usually on different teams or action groups. If you have house groups, put the clique members in one group. This can have a number of positive effects: it allows the rest of the group to develop relationships, it can speed up the group processes within the clique, and it can make the clique members keener to see other people when at the youth group, because they see enough of each other at the house group.

If, when you address the issue directly, members of the clique threaten to leave, say, 'Fine'. It is very important that we stand consistently for what we believe is right. One of the things I notice when reading the Gospels is that there were thousands around Jesus for the free lunches but when the teaching got tough, there weren't quite so many around and no one was keen to be crucified with him. If one young person is being picked on or is driven out of the group, we have to stand with that individual. It may mean sacrificing some of the more stubborn members of the group, but not usually. In the end you will be surprised because those who threatened to leave usually stay.

Lead by example We can be community builders by what we say and do. Young people will imitate us. We are role models and our example can be a great catalyst for good inward relationships.

Love The loving use of our time, the telephone call, the dinner invitation and the birthday card all help build relationships. Some of these kinds of things take up our time and our effort but they are well worth it.

Do things together in the programme Doing things together is extremely good for building up internal relationships. It creates bonds and relationships as well as shared experience and it breaks down barriers. Many of the Radical Action ideas (see chapter 5) have a spin-off benefit in group relationships, but weekends away, days out, activity challenges are also invaluable.

Never expect it to be perfect Youth work is always in a state of flux. The inward relationships are always dynamic. We need to roll with the ship sometimes rather than trying always to sail on the level. Be patient and don't be impulsive; sometimes time will sort things out as God gets to work in people's lives.

Disability challenge

- Divide your group into teams and give each team a programme card outlining your activities/sessions for the term, including social events.
- Allocate each group a disability: deaf, blind, dumb, wheelchair user, learning difficulties etc.
- Each team has to discuss how much a person who has their allocated disability would be able to participate in the group's programme: either fully, partially or not at all.
- Ask the teams to draw up a list of ideas or suggestions which might make the programme more accessible.
- Draw the teams back together and share the problems discovered by each team and then some of the solutions they have found.
- Use this session to make positive improvements to your programme. Even if you do not have any people with the allocated disabilities attending the group, positive use can be made of the exercise to look at our awareness of disability, the ways we exclude people who are different and what we can do to remedy it.

Thank yous to young people

Young people learn by example. If we appreciate them and show them real love and concern, eventually some of these principles will filter through into their own behaviour. It constantly amazes me (when I get time to think about it, and we all should do more of this) when I consider how much my young people actually give to me in so many different ways. As youth leaders it is good to say 'Thank you'. It may sound corny and obvious, but when done carefully it can have a huge effect on your young people. You can say thanks in a number of ways:

Say thanks with your time

- Invite young people round for food.

- Ring up to say, 'Well done', 'Thanks for clearing up' . . .
- Drop in a note to say, 'Thanks'.
- Listen to their stories, tales and problems to show you appreciate them.
- Buy them breakfast down at McDonald's or similar.

Say thanks with gifts

- Buy them a book or tape.
- Buy them a devotional poster.

Say thanks with prayer

- Ask them for lists of their exam times so you can pray. Ring them up afterwards to see how they went.
- Do pray . . . it's easy to forget when you are busy, but metaphorically 'tie' young people to things you do regularly. Pray for Nick and Joanne when you make coffee . . . Nicky and David when you get in the car . . . It may be that the only spare time you get is on the loo . . . but PRAY. Praying does make a difference!

Say thanks with your honesty

- If you are feeling low or upset, share your life and problems with certain young people. This has obviously to be done carefully, but they will see you as more human. We often feel as leaders that we have to be perfect: have a super-human devotional life, no money hassles and no problems or stresses generally. To share that you find reading the Bible difficult or that you have had the most dreadful day of your life can make a difference to the young person who also finds Bible reading difficult or who has also had a bad day. Don't do it all the time, but do give them a chance to minister to you! You may be surprised!

Say thanks with your sacrifices

Running a youth group isn't always easy:

- Prayer and counselling take time and make demands on us.

- Sharing your faults is difficult. I have often found, however, that my young people are all too often more than eager to share my faults with me!
- Sponsoring their fast (again) may cause you financial sacrifices.
- Having them all around for brekkie may put demands on your time.
- Discussing behaviour with the same individual (again) may place demands on your patience.
- Mopping up vomit after someone has got drunk and then come to youth group, or washing the shaving foam out of your car or hair or clothes . . . graffiti off walls . . . it goes on . . .

OUTWARD RELATIONSHIPS: BEYOND THE GROUP

Relationships with adults

This is one of the most important areas for developing relationships. Young people need to be able to interact with adult Christians who can provide much underutilized positive faith models.

Skills training Adults can sometimes have skills and abilities that your young people value and want, even if they are reluctant to admit that it is so. These skills can be in a variety of things. In one youth group, a police officer gave driving lessons to members of the group and let them use his car; in another group, basic car mechanics was being taught by a local garage owner and in another group, a young person taught his Vicar how to use a computer. Skills training can work both ways, and worthwhile and special relationships can be built between those who are sharing their expertise and those who are receiving.

Other valuable skills areas could involve:

Cooking when living on your own	Childcare
Motorbike servicing	Musical skills

Simple DIY   Money management
Craft activities   Youth work

Shadowing This is similar to skills training and is now quite often used for work experience, but it is still a valuable way of developing relationships between adults and young people. A young person shadows an adult through the working day, seeing what their work involves and how adults put their faith into action and relate their faith to their workplace. This is another excellent way of facilitating good relationships between the different age groups and the individual pairs involved.

House groups together If you have youth house groups and the adult congregation also has house groups, try combining two of the groups for a couple of meetings a year.

Use these meetings as an opportunity not just to learn about 'how the other half live', being the body of Christ or Titus 2:1–10, but also to value the fellowship and sharing. An evening could consist of fun warm-up activities, food, and the opportunity to chat etc.

Sporting activities The annual football match, cricket game, snooker or pool tournament sound dated but are excellent opportunities for adults and young people to get to know one another, not only during the game but also during the refreshments afterwards. Be inventive! Why not have a church bowling league or skittles evening? Perhaps combine outdoor summer sports with a fête or sponsored event. Why not challenge the adult men to paintballing or the congregation to a Lazerquest evening?

Relationships with children

Coaching session

In the same way that adults have skills to share with young

people, the young people themselves may have a huge number of skills which they can share with children.

Coaching children can be extremely hard work but also highly rewarding. Our young people's dance group was coached by an older young person and now they are helping some of our eight-to-ten-year-olds who are interested in exploring dance as a way of worshipping.

In addition to dance, skills can include anything: music, drama, football and sporty things, sewing and making clothes and banners, painting and arty things, and of course the inevitable help with homework.

Children's club (Sunday School, Junior Church . . .)

Many young people are exceptionally gifted with young children. They have an enthusiasm and ability to teach the Gospel in ways that we would never think of and sometimes cringe at! This can be valuable to everyone if the yong people are valued, trained and supported and not used as an easy and available labour force who will gradually 'grow up' to be with adults in the future.

Encouraging young people to help run these children's activities is excellent for:

- putting faith into action;
- building up relationships with and setting examples for children;
- helping young people vocalize and explain beliefs;
- fostering commitment and discipline.

Big brothers and sisters

All-age worship can be good for building up the family of God as everyone worships together; nevertheless it can be an absolute nightmare for the parents of small children. This is accentuated if one parent is involved in the worship group or other part of the service or is unable to be there.

We often have lots of teenagers in our services who occasionally (though not all the time as a cop-out from the worship!) act as 'big brothers and sisters' to those little ones. They can be someone other than their parents whom the little ones can sit next to, who they know will help them with the service and be their friend and role model.

We find that teens really enjoy not only the responsibility but also the company of the little ones in our services and the smaller ones build up attachments to the young people too. The little kids enjoy the opportunity to sit with someone else other than Mum or Dad sometimes, and it creates an opportunity for the parents to have a break and enjoy the service.

DOWNARDS RELATIONSHIPS: WITHIN OURSELVES

The fourth dimension for spiritual growth is down towards the centre of our own being. Christian faith can all too easily be a mask which young people put on in certain company. Downwards is where faith becomes 'grounded' and firmly based in the lives of the young people in our groups.

Encouraging this downward growth is not easy; it is a product of lots of other things that we do. Many of these things will occur in other parts of this book as faithbuilding is an integrated process: what we do, teach, model, pray, work at, explore and live out are all just parts of a process. Generally the downwards growth process itself may be helped along by our acceptance, our spirituality, worship and our availability.

Acceptance

We need to accept young people at the point where they are now and not wait until they are where we think they ought to be. God accepts them as they are and where they are. He knows if they only do their Bible reading once a month, he knows if you only do yours once a week, but he delights in this rather than sending us on a mega-guilt trip: he throws a party when you do it twice a week or they do it twice a month!

If we recognize how God accepts us and pass the acceptance on to our young people, they won't feel like they have to put on a religious 'super-Christian' mask or act to counteract the reality.

Spirituality

One of the best-selling Christian books of all time, after the Bible, is *The Imitation of Christ* by Thomas à Kempis. Our young people need to be imitators of Christ; not on the outside inwards but on the inside outwards.

So, what spiritual characteristics do we give most value to? Humility, self-sacrifice, patience, kindness? Or praying aloud, reading confidently, singing and playing guitar? The two sets are not, of course, mutually exclusive, but our ranking of their importance all too often is. This leads our young people to have the idea that what they do is more important than what they are, and this should be anathema to our youth ministry.

Worship

Worship is an opportunity to encounter God. As we give him the praise he is due, hear the Scriptures and pray together, we become open to the sanctifying power and presence of the Holy Spirit.

In worship, our young people can be converted, challenged and changed. Worship therefore is a vital ingredient to include in our programme and we should treat it with reverence and importance.

Availability

The times when young people want to talk about their inner struggles and experiences don't often coincide with our youth group meeting times and our availability to talk says that inner things are important and that the young people themselves are important. This encourages their confidence and helps them to continue to grow inwardly.

Session 1
WHAT HAVE I GOT TO OFFER?

AIM

To look at gifts and talents; to demonstrate that everyone has gifts and that they are all different.

PREPARATION

Equipment Group A	*Equipment Group B*
saucepan	large piece green oasis
bar of chocolate (4 oz)	skewer
rice crispies (4 oz)	knife
honey	
margarine	

WARM-UP

Divide your group into two smaller groups: Group A and Group B.

Group A

'Your task is to make chocolate crispy cakes using the ingredients laid out in the kitchen. Everyone must have a turn at making the cakes and there is enough of the ingredients to ensure that this happens. You do not have to wash up between each person but the kitchen will be inspected at the end of the exercise to ensure that everything is clean and tidy. Each person's cakes are to be placed on a plate at the side. You have ten minutes.'

Group B

'Your task is to each create a statue of the minister out of oasis using the knife and skewer provided.' [Provide a helpful picture pinned up on the wall.] You have ten minutes for the task.

After the ten minutes are up, gather the two groups back together and ask some people to show what they have done in the time given.

WORD-UP

How many people could make the chocolate crispy cakes?
Everyone.
How many people could sculpt the oasis? No one.

Everybody has gifts and talents. There are some things that
we can all do (and we'll be eating them later!) and some that
no one could do . . . (and we won't be eating them later).

ACTION

Pin up a piece of paper at each end of the room. Head one
of the pieces 'NATURAL TALENTS' and the other 'SPIRITUAL
GIFTS'. On a table in the middle of the room lay out a supply
of pens and green and yellow Post-it notes or sticky paper.

Members write any natural talents and spiritual gifts which
they can think of on the Post-it notes. (Green gifts and yellow
talents). These are then stuck onto the appropriate wall or
piece of paper.

Members may challenge whether they feel any particular
Post-it is an item which is a spiritual gift or a natural talent and
move it to the other wall. Allow for up to half a dozen
challenges.

Divide into groups of four and pass out Bible Study Cards.

Each group is to report back with their findings.

Ask each member to pick a gift and talent off the wall and to
go and put it on the back of a person in the group who they
think has that gift or talent.

NB There may be dangers with this exercise, so be aware of
what is happening in your group. Some people may receive
lots of Post-its and others none at all. This leaves young people
who feel that they really do have nothing to offer feeling worse,
but when a young person receives a Post-it unexpectedly
from another member they feel wonderfully affirmed and built
up. What will happen will obviously depend very much on
your group. If necessary, leaders could take part as givers
of Post-its but not as receivers, keeping an eye open for those

---

BIBLE STUDY CARD

1. What are the top five natural talents which the members of this group would like?

2. What are the top five spiritual gifts which the members of this group would like?

3. What were the gifts and talents God gave to His son in Isaiah 53:2–9 & Philippians 2:5–11?

4. Are there any gifts or talents which should be added to the walls tonight? Add them if you can think of any.

---

young people who are not on the receiving end.

When all the gifts and talents that can be, have been stuck on ... ask everyone to peel off the stickers they have received and read them.

Regather into one group or divide into small groups; ask people to give one word to describe how they feel. Look at the gifts and talents that are left on the wall.

TALK ABOUT

1. Why aren't these gifts represented in the group?
2. Should they be, and how could we draw in people who have these gifts or develop them in the members we have?

Session 2
CLIQUES

INTRODUCTION

You paint the picture for your group as follows:

'A youth group has decided to start two house groups so that young people may meet fortnightly on a Wednesday evening. These will be led by two of the couples who have been helping with the group on a Sunday evening. As the leader, you would like a good mixture of the committed and less committed, male and female and different ages in each group. Unfortunately, when you write a list of those who have said they are interested and added the information about the group members which you as leader have, your potential list of candidates for house groups looks something like this.'

The candidates

Matthew (17): Fancies Joanne but she does not appear interested.

Mark (15): Has just broken up with Mary after going out with her for six months; is eyeing up Helen.

Luke (15): Wants 'a laugh' and would like to be in the same group as Matthew whom he considers to be 'a laugh'.

John (14): Gets on well with Corinne and Phillipa: he looks up to them as being 'spiritually mature'.

Tim (18): Was friends with Matthew but he is now too busy and is looking for a girlfriend.

Corinne (18): Wants to be in a serious Bible study group and . . . 'do it properly'.

Phillipa (18): Best friends with Corinne and tries to do everything with her.

Joanne (17): Fancies Matthew but her parents don't want her to see him. The Minister has been told this and he has told you.

Justine (17): Doesn't want to be in the same group as her brother, John.

Mary (16): No one knows well, as she is new.

Rachel (15): Fancies Tim as does her friend Helen and you suspect she would like to use a house group as a chance to get to know him.

Helen (15): Is in the same class as Luke at school and thinks he is too immature.

Jose (15): Hates reading out loud and is very nervous indeed about joining a group.

Mary (14): Doesn't want to be in a group with any of the boys because of Mark.

TASK

In groups of four, put the candidates into two house groups which will meet the leaders' requirements and that will work. The groups are then to report back as to how they have allocated the candidates.

IN THE GROUPS

1. List your priorities for making the selections you did. What were the more important factors in your selections and what were the things that you did not take so much into account?

2. What do you feel was the members' first priority?

3. Do you think that the leaders set the right priorities?

4. In what ways is our group similar or different?

Session 3
LONELINESS

AIM

To create an opportunity for the young people to look at the issue of loneliness and some of the biblical responses to it.

INTRODUCTION

Today we are thinking about loneliness. We live in a society where loneliness is an epidemic: suicides, depression, alcohol and drug taking are all symptoms of the isolation and aloneness which many people experience as everyday.

Play 'Candle in the wind' by Elton John, which is about Marilyn Monroe.

WARM-UP

Lonely places

Where would you feel most alone?

(a) On your own on a wind-swept moor miles from anywhere and with the night coming down? *or*

(b) At a party where everyone is having a great time . . . except you?

Ask the group to go to the right-hand side of the room if they would feel more lonely in situation (a) and to the other side if they would be more lonely in situation (b).

Ask everyone in the group to find a partner (from the other side of the room, as far as is possible) and to spend one minute explaining to each other why they chose either option (a) or (b). In pairs, write a definition of loneliness in 20 words (maximum) on a sheet of paper that can then be put up onto the wall.

MAIN SESSION

Begin with passing out a LONELINESS SHEET to each person.

For each of the eight situations, each person gives a score ranging between 1 and 5: 1 is indicative of not feeling at all lonely and 5 being very lonely indeed. This score is entered into the first column.

The second column is a record of any situations that people can identify with as something they have already experienced.

After the exercise has been completed, ticks and scores are totalled and written in the TOTAL box at the bottom of the sheet. These two scores then combine to produce each person's loneliness ratio, e.g. if in the left-hand column a person scores 17 and also has 3 ticks in the right-hand column; their loneliness ratio will be 17:3. This ratio can then be produced in the form of a badge or sticker to be worn for the remainder of the session.

The loneliness ratio can make both members and leaders more aware of those who are suffering from loneliness and related problems. The ratios do not prove anything in themselves as it is quite possible to cheat. In a caring group, however, they can encourage those with pastoral gifts to befriend and talk with those who are lonely. It also brings out into the open things which we often keep hidden.

WORD-UP

Our loneliness ratio can be like our blood pressure, indicating if we are in need of looking after. In what ways could we help to bring each other's ratios down? Think of those inside the group and also those outside if you can.

Get into groups of five and produce a list of possibilities for action. Choose your top three.

REPORT BACK

After five minutes gather the groups back together and ask each group to report their top three possibilities. Put these on

LONELINESS

SITUATION	Score	Tick if this this has happened to you already
1. It is Saturday evening and you are stuck at home in front of the television.		
2. No one sits by you at lunch time.		
3. You ring a friend for a chat and they ask you to call back tomorrow.		
4. You are at home, sick for the third day in a row and no one from work, college or school called to ask how you are.		
5. You have been chosen for a local sports 1st team and try to tell your parents but they say that they're too busy to listen at the moment.		
6. At youth group no one notices that you are feeling down or comes over to talk to you especially.		
7. Your group of friends are going to a concert and haven't asked you.		
8. Everyone seems to be having a good time and you just don't feel part of what is going on.		
Score: 1 = not lonely 5 = very lonely		
TOTAL		

an overhead projector or flip chart so that everyone can see them.

BIBLE INVESTIGATION

In pairs look at some of the things that God has to say about being alone and loneliness. (Don't give out verses to the groups unless they are stuck.) Ask the group:

Where would you start?

What verses or passages would you give to a lonely friend?

How should the Church care more for people who are lonely?

WORD-UP

After ten minutes have the pairs share with the group some of the things they have discovered and some of their thoughts.

Session 4
IT'S OUR GROUP

One of the dangers often with youth groups is that they can become cliques; introverted and not at all welcoming to strangers.

AIM

To look at some of the prejudices that may stop new young people joining your group.

WARM-UP

Divide the group into two: give each sub-group flip chart paper and a pen.

Group A should brainstorm as many ways as they can think of that people are different.

Group B should brainstorm as many ways as they can think of that people are the same.

Give the group about three minutes to do this. At the end of the time gather the two groups back together and share what they have come up with. See if the groups can define any of these areas within their lists:

- Physical differences, similarities (denote as P)
- Mental differences, similarities   (denote as M)
- Emotional differences, similarities (denote as E)
- Spiritual differences, similarities (denote as S)
- Relational differences, similarities (denote as R)

WORD-UP

There are some things we all have in common as *people* but there are also many, many differences between us. Let us imagine the nightmare scenario: what could that person who turns up to youth group out of the blue . . . really be like?

MAIN SESSION

Divide pieces of A4 paper down their longest length and hand out half a sheet and a pencil to everyone in the group.

Explain that you are going to play a game of 'Nightmare Consequences'.

You are going to call out a characteristic: at which point everyone is to write down, at the top of their paper, a corresponding description of the person they would least like to turn up to youth group.

The paper is then folded over to conceal what was written and passed on to the next person who fills in the next characteristic. The paper could end up looking something like this:

1. Male or female?	1. Male
2. Hair colour?	2. Purple, mohican
3. Clothes?	3. From C&A
4. Music taste?	4. Take That! fan
5. Interests?	5. Stamp collecting, snail racing
6. Family background?	6. Father is the Vicar
7. Where do they live?	7. On the estate

8. Personal history?	8. Never done anything
9. Education?	9. 5 A levels, 13 GCSEs
10. Spiritual life? (adapt to suit your group)	10. Born again, hell-fire evangelist type.

When all the characteristics have been completed the last person folds over the paper and passes it on. The next person can open up the paper and everyone shares their nightmare person with the rest of the group, usually with hilarious results.

WORD-UP

We joked a lot about the profiles of our nightmare people as we read them out to each other. However, someone in the group may have one or a number of the characteristics which come out in the game. If this does happen, pick this up and challenge the group in the word-up section. Quite often what seems a painful or unkind experience can, with good and sensitive leadership, turn out to be a growth point. This exercise only uncovers the prejudices which are already there. To imagine that these do not exist just because they have not been aired is naïve and unhelpful.

Let's have a look at how Jesus coped with people who were considered to be nightmare people or outcasts by the society in which they lived.

BIBLE INVESTIGATION

Group A: John 9:1–34

A blind outcast

1. In what ways was the man an outcast from society? A nightmare person?
2. What do you think was the cause of the man's blindness?
3. How did Jesus treat the man?
4. How did the religious leaders treat the man?

5. What lessons can we learn from this?

Group B: Luke 8:30–50

An outcast with a reputation

1. In what ways was the woman an outcast from society and a nightmare person?
2. What were the steps the woman had to take and the costs she had to pay in approaching Jesus?
3. How did Jesus treat the woman?
4. How did the Pharisees react to and treat the woman?
5. What lessons can we learn from this?

Group C: Luke 19:1-11

An unpopular outcast

1. In what ways was the man an outcast?
2. What could have been the motivation behind his behaviour, do you think?
3. How did Jesus treat the man?
4. How did the people react to Jesus' treatment of the man?
5. What lessons can we learn from this?

Group D: John 4:4-30

A racial outcast

1. Why was the woman an outcast?
2. In what ways do you think the woman avoided Jesus?
3. How did Jesus treat the woman?
4. What were the disciples' reactions to Jesus' interaction with the woman?
5. What lessons can we learn from this?

Sound back

Allow the groups time to report back, especially on questions 2, 3 and 5.

GOING FURTHER

Putting it into practice

How can we be more welcoming as a group and reflect Jesus in the way we treat people? Have two members read out loud James 2:1–7 and 1 John 3:16–20.

Now ask the group to divide into pairs and consider the following, point 1 as a pair and points 2 and 3 in groups of several pairs.

1. Each pair is to draw up five commandments for the group's attitude and treatment of those who are outside the group.

2. Join three or four pairs together to produce a 'Top Ten' out of the commandments (depending of course on group size). Write these onto sheets of paper.

3. Put up the sheets on the wall. Members are to vote for the group's Top Ten and these are then written down. These can then be typed up and given to members as a reminder of what was decided when they meet the next time.

Session 5
THE GREAT YOUTH CLUB DISASTER

AIM

To work together as a group on problem solving.

PREPARATION

Photocopy the key facts and cut the paper into strips so that each of the individual 'Key Facts' is on an individual strip of paper.

THE GENERAL SCENE

It's Monday morning and the Youth Minister has discovered that the video, TV and all the Mars Bars are missing from the club.

The Youth Minister rings all the leaders to find out what they have to say but owing to an extremely bad line he only gets down part of what they all said.

The Pastor has asked the Youth Minister to come to him and explain in an hour's time, and he has already used up half an hour writing up the key facts.

THE TASK

Your task is to try and work out what happened on Sunday night and how the place was robbed without any sign of a forced entry.

Each person will be given a number of 'Key Facts'.
You cannot show your pieces of paper to anyone.
You can only share their contents by reading them out to the group.
You have thirty minutes to solve the mystery.

KEY FACTS

1. There were five leaders on duty on Sunday night.
2. Each leader had a different responsibility.
3. Only the two senior leaders had keys.
4. The two senior leaders had sole responsibility for locking up.
5. There was only one male senior leader.
6. The fire exit, when closed, could only be opened from the inside.
7. The kitchen hatch was closed when the club was closed.
8. The youth club had three exits.
9. The main exit leads onto Old Church Road.
10. The church front door had to be opened and closed with a key.
11. The door from the club to the church could be opened from the club side, without a key.
12. The leader who washed up left third at 10.15 pm.
13. One person let himself or herself out through the church.

14. Hannah's car was parked on the Main Street until 10.10 pm.
15. The tuckshop cashier drove home first.
16. The leader who washed up left through the fire exit.
17. Two leaders chatted in the kitchen about the evening until 10.20 pm.
18. David was home before the late movie started. The late movie started at 10.15 pm.
19. Someone re-entered through the main exit to collect their coat.
20. John was the last to drive home.
21. It took five minutes for the leader who washed up to find his coat in church.
22. The leader who tidied the games equipment never wore a coat.
23. A senior leader checked the club and locked the main door as he left.
24. Peter left through the main exit.
25. Two people used the fire exit.
26. Only two leaders drove to church.
27. Rebecca usually went for a run after club.
28. The leader who tidied the games equipment left through the fire exit.
29. Peter left the door open when he left.

CORRECT SOLUTION

Peter washed up and then left through the main exit at 10.15 pm.

He returned to the club to find his coat which was in church. By the time that he had found his coat, the club had been locked up and everyone had gone home.

He left through the fire exit and forgot to shut it properly.

DEBRIEFING

If the group have found a solution, tell them if it is correct and move on to the debrief. If their solution is not the correct one, either give them a little more time to explain what the solution is before moving on to the de-brief.

- How do you feel?
- How did the group go about completing the task?
- Who did what in the group?
- Who took the lead?
- Who hindered the result?
- Who was the quietest person?
- What was necessary for the puzzle to be solved?
- Were any assumptions made in finding the solution?
- How can we apply the process of puzzle solving to this group?

GOING FURTHER

In reality, the removal of some of the material possessions of the youth club is not such a disaster. There are other things, however, that could happen that would be a real youth group disaster:

- What would be a real disaster for this group?
- What action could we take after the disaster or should we take after the disaster?
- Are there disasters happening already that we do not see?
- What was the biggest disaster in Jesus' life and ministry? Why?

Session 6

REJECTION

AIM

To look at what happens when you are hurt by someone who rejects you and how we are to respond to this as Christians.

EQUIPMENT AND PREPARATION

Lots of balloons, felt-tip pens.

WARM-UP

There are several good games that can be used as a warm-up for this session, e.g. 'Smash yer face in', 'Find a partner', and 'Break in/Break-out'.

WARM-UPS

Smash yer face in!

1. Give each person a balloon and a felt pen. They should blow up their balloon, tie it and then draw a face on it to represent how they feel at that moment.

2. When everyone has drawn the face on their balloon, go round the circle and have everyone introduce their 'face' to the rest of the group.

3. Everyone then places their balloon on the floor in the middle of the room and goes and stands round the edge of the room.

4. As the command 'GO!' is given, everyone has to try to protect their 'face' without using their hands or picking it up off the floor and at the same time try to burst other people's faces.

5. After thirty seconds, yell 'STOP!' and see how many people are left with a 'face' still intact.

6. Instant share: go round the circle again and say one word which describes how you feel.

Find a partner

Make lots of small slips of paper and put them into pairs. On both pieces of each pair, write the name of an animal, shape, vegetable, vehicle, film star . . . anything providing it is always the same as its pair. When you have finished there will be two of everything. However, on one or two pieces of paper (depending whether there is an odd or an even number of people playing) put the name of something or someone that is unpaired.

Fold the pieces of paper in half and place them all in a large container. Ensure that there are exactly the same number of pieces of paper as there will be people playing the game. It is worth having a couple of extra ones just in case someone turns up a little late.

1. Everyone in the group draws out a slip of paper and reads what is on it.

2. In silence, the group has to mime (all at the same time) their animal, vehicle, vegetable or whatever and try to find their partner.

3. If there is an odd number of people playing do make sure that there are NOT three of a kind. If you are playing with an even number of participants ensure that there is an odd pair. So there might be an odd potato and an odd radish left at the end, for example.

4. Someone (or two someones if you began with an even number) at the end of the game will, therefore, be left without a partner.

5. To be really cruel and accentuate the point of the exercise, before the game begins, tell everyone that when they have found their partner, they are to go and sit round the room. Inevitably, at the end, one or two people will be left in the middle of the room doing their mime.

Break in/Break out

These games are also excellent warm-ups for this session.

Divide the group into smaller groups of about six to eight members. Ask for a volunteer from each group.

The remaining group members stand in a circle around the volunteer and link arms to make a secure circle around the volunteer in the middle.

The person standing in the middle of the circle has to try to BREAK OUT! of the circle by any means possible.

BREAK IN! happens as above but the other way round: The volunteer stands outside the circle and tries to BREAK IN! using any means possible.

After the volunteers have had a go and succeeded or failed, let others who want to have a go at either variation to experience what it feels like.

Ask the members who tried to break in or to break out:

- Which was easier: breaking in or breaking out?
- What did the experience feel like?
- What did it feel like to be excluded?
- Did anything that happened in the game make it easier or harder to cope with?

WORD-UP

Feeling embarrassment or rejection and being trapped are some of the situations which cause us to be hurt. Here's a story about being hurt, at the end of which we are going to look at who was hurt by whom, how and why:

Andy and Dave had been best friends for years and years. In fact they had been friends since they started secondary school. They had got on well and were now members of their local Church Youth Fellowship.

Then it happened. Andy met Clare. She was new to church, full of life and for some reason Andy just wanted to spend loads of time with her. They didn't really do anything, just chatted and spent time together.

One day, Dave and Andy decided to go down to the pub the following Friday evening to catch up on the news, but Andy's mind was elsewhere, especially when Clare suggested that Andy and she should spend a quiet night watching the latest video release at her place.

On Friday night, Dave sat in the pub staring wistfully at his drink wondering where Andy could be, and also feeling embarrassed and let down.

The next Sunday after church, Dave had a word with Clare's best friend, Fiona, to express his worries. 'Andy and Clare are seeing so much of each other: he was round there on Friday night and I'm worried that they might be sleeping together.'

Fiona was consequently worried too. She really liked Clare and didn't want to see her ruin her life and wreck her relationship with God. So, she did the Christian thing and invited four of her friends to pray for Clare after they had talked over the kinds of things that they should pray and how Clare was sleeping with Andy. They told God all the gossip.

Next day at college, one of the friends who had been in the prayer group saw Clare and told her that they were all praying for her the night before so that she would have the spiritual strength to stop sleeping with Andy. Clare was furious and assumed that Andy was behind the rumour. She stormed up to him and said she never wanted to see him again.

When you have read the story, either go over the details again or pass out photocopies of it so that everyone can read it.

Hand out a REJECTION SHEET (as below) to everyone and ask them to think about the story and then fill in their sheet.

For the behaviour rank column: put a 1 next to the person who behaved the best. A 2 next to the person who behaved second best and so on through to a mark of 5 for the person who behaved the worst. For the hurt rating: give each person a mark out of 10 to represent how hurt you think they are, 10 being extremely hurt and 1 being not hurt at all.

REJECTION SHEET		
NAME	*BEHAVIOUR*	*HURT RATING*
DAVE		
ANDY		
CLARE		
FIONA		
FRIENDS		

When everyone has completed their sheets have the group report back.

CONCLUSION

Consider the following questions in the whole group.

What would have been better action by the people in the story?

Why is it that we often don't act as we should but act like the characters did?

What can we do to help the relationships in our group so that these kinds of situations do not arise?

Session 7
SHARING EXERCISE

AIM

To encourage members of the group to share with each other and feel more comfortable doing so.

PREPARATION

Photocopy enough copies of 'The Drawing Room' for everyone to have a copy.

ACTION

1. Pass out a copy of 'The Drawing Room' to everyone.

2. Everyone should put their own name next to the description which they think best fits them and the names of two other group members against the description which they think most fits them.

After everyone has filled in their own name against a description and the names of two other group members, divide into groups of four or five to share answers.

Ask these questions in small groups:

- Why have you put yourself where you are?
- Why did you put the others where you put them?

Bring the small groups back together and as a large group share parts of the small groups' discussions. Members may share with the whole group where they put themselves and where others put them if they wish.

Try to draw out if people were happy with where their peers put them in the scenario or whether they were unhappy. The conversation should be one of affirmation and acceptance.

Ask together:

- How well did we know each other?
- What could we do to develop the relationships within the group?

THE DRAWING ROOM

COAL BUCKET: Forgotten except when the group needs warming up or somewhere to put the rubbish	
FIREPLACE: A warming influence on the group but if people get too close they may get burnt.	
GRAND PIANO: A pose in the corner but your gifts do not get used	
OLD GRAMOPHONE: Full of good things but rarely listened to	
READING LIGHT: Try to illuminate the area around you but don't seem to make much progress	
ROCKING CHAIR: Everyone's favourite place to be	
SETTEE: You feel kicked, battered and squashed by everyone but at least you are involved	
BOOKSHELF: Full of information and facts	
ARMCHAIR: Cosy person but a bit of a loner	
HEARTH RUG: Worn out and trodden upon by everyone but still looks good	

Make a list of the suggestions and choose some to put into action.

CONCLUSION

Close with a time of open prayer, allowing members to pray quietly or aloud as they wish, giving thanks for each other and the gifts and contributions they all bring to the group.

FOUR

Relevant Teaching

Who is God anyway?

INTRODUCTION

This module examines four key elements of the question: 'Who is God anyway?'

1. How do we know about God?
2. What is God like?
3. What has God got against sin?
4. Why does God allow suffering?

Of course these are only a few of the many questions that we could ask here, but these four in particular were chosen because they relate specifically to four 'bases' or 'foundations' essential when helping young people to faith.

1. How do we know about God? This explores the nature of revelation and so leads us to the fact that it *is* possible to know God and have a relationship with Him.

2. What is God like? This looks at the character of God and demonstrates the difference between God's values and the world's values. This progresses to an understanding of God's concern for the world and opens up a need for action.

3. What has God got against sin? This centres on the issue of personal sin and the need to deal with sin before we can have a relationship with God and come into his presence. It explores the significance of Christ's death on the Cross.

4. Why does God allow suffering? This opens up the idea that Christianity has a 'here and now' dimension as well as an eternal one and tries to grapple with some of the questions that suffering raises.

Common questions

In the course of teaching young people on the issues contained in this module, you may come across the following questions or misconceptions. Some preparation and thought about these will help you decide the best ways in which to deal with the issues raised, either within the relevant session or at some other appropriate time.

- If God is loving, why does He send people to hell?
- If God is supposed to be just, why is life so unfair?
- Was Jesus God – or was he just a godly man?
- How can God be interested in knowing me?
- How can we know *anything* about God at all?
- Christianity might work for you but it's not right for me.

Book resources

The Bible; *Knowing God* by J I Packer; *Lion Handbook of Christian Belief*; *Fear no Evil* by David Watson; *Joni* by Joni Earikson; *Understanding the Trinity* by Alistair Mcgrath

Session 1
HOW DO WE KNOW ABOUT GOD?

AIM

To discover that Christianity is about God's revelation of himself through Jesus. We are looking at how we can know God or how God makes himself known to us.

WARM-UP

Choose either option (a) or option (b) and follow either with 'word-up'.

Option (a): Sensing tests

These look at how we experience things in the world around us in everyday life. You will need four tables with various objects on them relating to one of the senses (sound, taste, smell and touch).

Table 1: Sound This table has four personal stereos on it. In each stereo should be a tape with a series of strange noises on it for the listener to identify. Sounds could include a kettle boiling, a car starting, a drawer opening, tap dripping – be inventive!

Table 2: Taste This table holds four plates, each with white powder on it for the young people to identify. The powders could include things such as plain flour, self-raising flour, baking powder, icing sugar, cornflour, etc.

Label the powders A, B, C and D, and provide glasses of water for each taster.

Table 3: Smell This table should have four bowls labelled P, Q, R and S. Each one should have a different stick deodorant in it. Use both male and female varieties and remove the labels. The contestants have to try and identify each one.

Table 4: Touch Here the contestants will need to be blindfolded before the items are placed on the table. The contestants have to try to identify by touch a number of plastic model farmyard animals or something similar. Label these W, X, Y and Z.

ACTION

Divide the group into teams of four at the beginning.

Each team takes its turn to visit each table and do the tasks one by one.

If you have a large group you will need to have either more tables or larger teams who nominate four players to play each challenge. Each contestant will need a score sheet similar to that below. You can adapt the form to suit your own challenges or photocopy the one provided.

THE SENSE TEST	
TOUCH	LISTEN
W	Sound 1 ....
X	Sound 2 ....
Y	Sound 3 ....
Z	Sound 4 ....
SMELL	TASTE
P	A ....
Q	B ....
R	C ....
S	D ....

When all the teams have completed the exercise above, gather everyone back together and read out the answers to THE SENSE TEST so that everyone can know, for fun, who the winners were.

Then, divide into small groups (try not to include members from the same teams used for the above in the same group).

Ask each group to answer the questions below:

- Why were some of the tests easier to do than others?
- How did you know what things were?
- In what ways is identifying an object different to identifying a person?

Option (b): On the couch...

Setting the scene Set up one end of the room to look like an archetypal nineteenth-centry psychiatrist's room. Use a couch (tables covered in a blanket perhaps?), chairs, desk, standard lamp, etc. You could also dress up the psychiatrist with a white coat, round glasses, etc. Use as much or as little in the way of props as you wish.

Prepare two older young people or leaders beforehand so they have time to practise their roles as psychiatrist or client.

The psychiatrist is trying to find out information from the client, e.g. 'What did you do on your tenth birthday?' and 'What do you hope to be doing in two years' time?'

The client is free to volunteer information or not; the client can be evasive or sidetrack. Allow the conversation to develop. Maybe you could have two or three different situations and clients if you wish. Although this won't be read out when the sketch begins it should be made clear that the psychiatrist has a letter about the client (probably from the client's doctor).

Then divide the group into threes or fours and hand out or put up on the overhead the following questions:

- How did we know if the client was telling the truth?
- What did the psychiatrist do to encourage the client to share the information?
- Would it have been easier for the psychiatrist if he or she had known the client for a long time?
- Were there any other sources of information the psychiatrist could have drawn on to help the client?

Give the groups about ten minutes to answer the questions and appoint a spokesperson to report back.

REPORT BACK

Allow each of the groups to report back, noting the facts for use in the summing-up section.

SUM UP

The psychiatrist could draw on three sources of information in his or her discussion with the client:
- the information the client shares;
- any information or evidence he has obtained elsewhere (e.g. from doctor's reports);
- the evidence of his own relationship with the client (i.e. the psychiatrist can ask: 'Is the information shared by the client consistent with the person I know and the information previously shared?'

WORD-UP

We can know about God in three ways: revelation, testimony and experience.

1. Revelation The information he reveals to us. We will look at how he reveals himself a bit later on.

2. Testimony This is the experience of others who are witnesses to the things God has done.

3. Experience The evidence of our own relationship with God: i.e. is this consistent with my experience of God?

BIBLE INVESTIGATION

Divide into small groups and give each group one of the following Bible passages to look at and a set of instructions:

Hebrews 1:1–4
Psalm 111
Psalm 139: 1–16
2 Timothy 3: 14–17

1 Samuel 3: 1–11
Isaiah 6: 1–10
John 8: 42–47 (for older groups only)

Instructions Read the passage through carefully. Use different Bible translations if you find that helpful in understanding the passage.
1. List the different ways in which God reveals himself in the passage.
2. Does God still reveal himself this way today?

Report back

Let the groups report back and list on a large sheet of paper or the overhead projector the ways in which God may reveal himself. Next to each item you can put a tick or a cross depending on whether the group feels God uses that method today.

WORD-UP

Explain that God is a God who reveals himself.

Christianity is a faith concerned not with us seeking after God but *God* seeking after us.

Session 2
WHAT IS GOD LIKE?

AIM

To discover that Christianity is about God's revelation of himself through Jesus.

WARM-UPS

Card characteristics

A fun game to familiarize young people with some of the characteristics of God.

Preparation

Make a pack of cards. Use plain cards as you will be writing a characteristic of God on each card. Write each characteristic on four cards. So, you might have four cards saying, *Judge*, four saying *Creator*, four cards saying *Sustainer*, etc. Other characteristics you could use include *Lord, Father, Redeemer, Eternal, Merciful, Just, Big*...

You will also need some spoons: one less spoon than there are players.

Action

The players sit in a circle and the spoons are placed in the middle of the circle.

Shuffle the cards you made earlier and deal four to each player. The object of the game is to collect all four cards with the same characteristic.

All players simultaneously pass one card to the left on the command 'change'. As soon as one person has four cards that are the same, he or she calls out what the characteristic is and grabs for a spoon.

This is the signal for everyone else in the game also to make a grab for a spoon. The person who doesn't manage to get one in the scrum loses a point.

Play several rounds; the losers can wash up.

Canned curiosity

How do we know what something is like without experiencing it in an 'edible' sort of way?

Preparation

Carefully remove the labels off a variety of unopened tinned foods (tomatoes, baked beans, chick peas, soup, stewed prunes, etc). Keep the labels and mark the tins with a letter so you can identify which tin is which.

Action

Divide the group into teams, give each team a set of weighing scales, the tins and the labels: the team must try to identify each of the tins without opening them and then choose one to eat.

When the teams have made their guesses invite them out one at a time to the front for the ceremonial opening and eating of the contents.

MAIN SESSION: USE EITHER OPTION (a)
OR OPTION (b)

Option (a): What if ...?

Aim

To encourage thought on whether the existence of God may be an influence on society.

Action

Divide the group into threes and pass out a WHAT IF? sheet to each of the small groups.

Allow about ten minutes to talk it through.

One person from each three should be ready after this time to report back.

WHAT IF? . . .

Imagine a society where there is no God. He does not exist. 'Here and now' is all that there is.

What might life be like for a person your age in that society? It may help you to think of some of the following:

Reasons for living, sex, values, love, death, fear, art, attitudes to others.

Option (b): What is love?

Aim

We talk about the character of God as being *just* or *loving*, but what does this really mean? This section of Session 1 helps young people to begin thinking about this issue.

Action

Divide the group into four equal teams: A, B, C and D. If possible send each team to a different place to work. If this is not possible you could use the corners of the room.

In the centre of the room place all the youth group's art and craft supplies, clay remnants, junk material, etc. This is the 'equipment pool'.

Give each team one of the instruction cards and the equipment named on it.

Check on the groups as they do the investigation and give them a bit of help if they get stuck. At the end of the time draw them back together and take the presentations one at a time.

After all the groups have presented, brainstorm the differences between what the Bible says and what society says onto a flip chart or overhead projector.

TEAM A

Your task is to investigate what 'love' means in today's society as demonstrated in the music magazines and newspapers you have been given.

Equipment: Cassette player, teenage and young adult magazines, tabloid newspapers.

You have twenty minutes to make your investigation, then fifteen minutes to plan and prepare how to present this material to the rest of the group. You can use any of the equipment that you have in your group or the equipment pool.

TEAM B

Your task is to investigate the biblical meaning of the word 'love'.

You have the following equipment to help you: Bibles (various translations), a concordance, a Bible dictionary, a hymn book and a chorus book (music edition).

You have twenty minutes to make your investigation, then fifteen minutes to plan and prepare a presentation to the rest of the group. You may use any of your own equipment plus any from the equipment pool.

TEAM C

Your task is to investigate what is meant by 'justice' in today's society as demonstrated by the music magazines and newspapers you have been given.

You have the following equipment to help you: magazines and newspapers including 'Smash Hits' (or a similar one containing lyrics to current songs).

You have twenty minutes to make the investigation then fifteen minutes to prepare a presentation to the rest of the group. You can use any of your own equipment or any in the equipment pool.

TEAM D

Your task is to investigate what is meant by 'justice' in the Bible.

You have the following equipment to help you: Bibles (various translations), a concordance, a Bible dictionary, a hymn book, and a chorus book (music edition).

You have twenty minutes to make the investigation then fifteen minutes to plan and prepare a presentation to the rest of the group. You can use any of your own equipment plus any from the equipment pool.

WORD-UP

When we talk about God being 'Love' or God being 'Just' it is important that we don't define those words as they are commonly used today. We must discover what they really mean in the Bible or how we see them demonstrated in Jesus' life.

OPEN FLOOR

Have an open discussion on the following questions and issues:

- To what extent can our finite minds know an infinite God?
- Knowing God personally is only possible for a Christian.
- The character of God is never changing.
- God loves us enough to 'punish' us?

NB. The Bible investigations above used the concepts of God as Love and Justice. The same investigations, of course, may be used to look at any of the other characteristics of God depending on the slant which you may wish to give your session, e.g.

- God as Peace
- God as Creator
- God as Holy
- God as Good
- God as Forgiving

Session 3
WHAT HAS GOD GOT AGAINST SIN?

AIM

To look at the nature of sin: why does it separate us from a holy God and what has God done to make it possible to restore our relationship with Him?

WARM-UP

Choose one or a combination of the following exercises ('Mastermind', 'Ball Chuck' and 'Circle pull'), or you may prefer to invent a similar game to make the point.

Mastermind

Set up an area like the programme *Mastermind*: include chair, lights etc and call out contestants one at a time. Each contestant has two minutes to answer questions.

You could write your own questions (on any subject) or borrow from any quiz game; it is important that the questions should be difficult so that no contestant is likely to get every one correct.

Allow four or five players to have a go.

Ball chuck

Set up a bucket about five metres from a chair.

Contestants have to stand on the chair and throw tennis balls into the bucket. The contestant keeps on throwing until a ball either misses the bucket or bounces out of it. The contestant scores the number of balls in the bucket at the end of his turn.

Circle pull

Draw a chalk circle on the floor using a diameter of 10 cm for every person playing. (For example, if there are twenty-five players, the circle will be 2.5 m in diameter.) All players hold hands in a circle around the chalk one.

The object is to pull other players inside the chalk circle while remaining outside it yourself. Anyone treading inside the chalk circle is eliminated, and if two players let go hands in the struggle which follows, both are also out.

MAIN SESSION

Choose either option (a) or option (b) for the main body of this session:

Option (a): Sin-stained shirts

Divide the group into threes. Each group of three is given a cheap, large white T-shirt (or group members could bring their own) and marker pens.

The group write on the T-shirt every sin which they can think of in a given time limit and then one of the group models the finished result.

Allow everyone to look at all the shirts and then have the shirt-wearers line up at the front for the whole group to vote on the 'biggest sinner'. Note the top three vote-winners.

Explain that each of the top three vote-winners has been invited to a party but it is, unfortunately, a white-shirt event and none of them is likely to get in, owing to their present state.

To help the situation offer the shirt-wearers bottles of Tipp-Ex, or a bucket of water perhaps, to cover up their sins. To the winner of the vote you could give a bag of soap powder with a bucket of water, as a special treat!

The shirt-wearers have five minutes to make their shirt presentable for the party – let them draw on the help of the whole group if necessary. After the five minutes are up, ask them to remodel their shirts.

You can comment:

- Hold up a Tipp-Exed shirt: 'Trying to cover up our sins is really no solution; it does not solve the problem of the sins themselves, merely tries to disguise them . . . badly. We are still not presentable.'
- Hold up the wet shirt: 'Trying to clean up our own act to make us presentable for the party is no help either . . . we can't get rid of the stains that sin leaves.'
- Hold up the washing-powdered shirt: 'Even man-made solutions don't solve the problem completely. The problem may seem to have faded, but it is still there. Still not presentable enough for the party I'm afraid . . .'
- 'The Bible says, "If anyone is in Christ, they are a new creation. The old has gone . . ." When God cleanses us from our sins, he doesn't cover them over, he doesn't leave the job half done and us all stained . . . he makes us like a brand new shirt.'

Take all the stained shirts and put them on a large cross. Give out clean shirts to everyone.

Hold a celebration meal (see food section).

Option (b): Weaving the sin web

Divide the group into four teams and give each team a reel of cotton, Post-it stickers of two different colours, paper, pencils and some Blu-Tack.

Each of the teams has to list all the different sins in the world that it can think of. (If yours is a young group, perhaps give them a few newspapers to help them a little.)

For each of the sins which they have named, they need to ask themselves if it is an 'individual' sin or a 'societal' sin. Give a few examples as below:

Personal sin	*Societal sin*
stealing	injustice
murder	war
greed	greed

The personal sins are allocated one of the Post-it colours and the societal sins the other. The sins are then written onto the appropriate Post-its and stuck to the wall.

When as many sins as possible in the time allocated have been stuck to the wall, it is time to begin making connections between the sins, e.g. there could be a connection between greed and injustice, such as paying low wages so that products may be obtained more cheaply, between stealing and murder or mugging, and so on.

Connections are made between the Post-it stickers using the cotton. Each connection should be explained with a label. As the connections begin to build up on the wall, a tangled web will begin to emerge.

Give the groups about thirty to forty minutes for the whole exercise, depending on age and ability.

WHY DOES GOD ALLOW SUFFERING?

AIM

To look at the question of suffering in the light of a God that is Good.

WARM-UP

Select either option (a) or option (b), or use both if there is time!

Option (a): Looking behind the headlines

Divide the group into four teams; each team is given a question sheet and one of the following:

- a selection of local newspapers
- a selection of quality newspapers
- a video of the evening news
- a tape of various radio news broadcasts.

QUESTION SHEET

1. What different types of suffering are reported in your news?
2. What are the possible causes of this suffering?
3. Are there any solutions to these which are given by the news broadcast?

After fifteen minutes gather the groups back together and share together the answers to the first two questions on their question sheet.

Option (b): Peg it!

Each player has six clothes pegs, and the objective of the game is simple: to peg all your clothes pegs onto any of the other players while avoiding getting pegged yourself. (Pegging them onto other players is the only way that players can get rid of their pegs.)

Once they have pegged away their original six pegs, players may start removing the ones pegged on to them by pegging other people.

After three minutes, stop the game.

Ask the contestants to line up in order, according to the number of pegs they have on them.

Invite three winners (those who have the fewest pegs) out to the front. The losers are the winners' slaves for the remainder of the session.

MAIN SESSION PART 1

AIM

To investigate any possible connection between sin and suffering.

ACTION

Divide the group into pairs and give out the following letter to each pair.

Dear John,

I'm sorry that I have to write to you but I could not tell you face to face. I have found someone else. Well, you found him really, as it's Peter, your best friend.

We've been going out for two months now, but I really didn't want to hurt you so we sort of put off telling you. It's not that I don't love you; it's just that I love him more. I know you'll understand.

I don't think that I could ever be just good friends so it would be best if you never spoke to me again.

Love Jane.

Give each pair time to read the letter and then give them the following questions:

1. Rank each of the three characters' behaviour, 1 being the worst and 3 being the best.

Peter:....................................

John:....................................

Jane: ....

2. What do you think are the causes of each character's situation?

3. Can you think of other examples in your experience where sin leads to suffering?

4. Can you think of examples in the world where sin leads to suffering?

Let the groups come back together to share their findings.

MAIN SESSION: PART 2

AIM

To investigate what suffering actually is and how we come to this definition.

ACTION

Instead of using the obvious beginning (pictures of starving children, war victims or refugees), start by using either pictures or video clips of the exact opposite: rich people, big houses, fast cars . . . any 'brat pack' movie will have plenty, for example.

Divide the group into pairs and ask each pair to list three things that they find most attractive about the lifestyle portrayed.

List the answers on an overhead projector or flip chart, repeating the answers that come up more than once so the most popular ones can be easily identified.

Taking each of the top few characteristics in turn, ask the whole group to divide to one side of the room or the other according to whether they think that to do without such an article would be suffering; e.g. if a characteristic is 'never having to worry about money', people have to move to the left of the room if they feel that to do without money is suffering or to the right if they feel the opposite.

After the last item has been called, ask the pairs to join together to make groups of four and to produce their own definition of suffering.

When all groups have finished, one person from each group of four reads out their definition.

Now, play a second set of video clips, using footage of war zones, famine, natural disasters, poverty, etc.

In groups of four, share answers and reactions to the following:

1. In the videos, what did you find the most disturbing?
2. Which of these would you *least* like in your life?
3. In what ways is your definition of suffering (from earlier) inadequate in the light of the pain and suffering in the world of the people in the video clips?
4. Are we, as Western Christian young people, less able to cope with suffering and pain compared with our Christian brothers and sisters elsewhere?

OPEN FLOOR

Have an open discussion based on the following questions.

- What do we mean by 'fair'? Must our concept of 'fair' alter if we think about life having an eternal dimension?
- If God is totally 'just', what can we make of the present state of the world?
- *As a challenge*: Are there characteristics in our behaviour towards people of different class, sex, ability, culture, etc, which are indicative of the unfair treatment they receive at the hands of society?

PRAYERS

Sometimes words are not enough – they don't express the pain and anger which we want to shout at God when we see or experience some of the things that will have arisen in this session on suffering. The Bible tells us of people weeping, wailing, fasting, praying prostrate on the ground, tearing their clothes and screaming and shouting to God in prayer.

We need to encourage our young people to be honest and open in their prayers. Here are some thoughts on how to help young people to begin exploring this idea in their prayers and worship:

- Nail newspaper articles to a cross (you will need a large cross and nails): the act of nailing the articles to the cross is a way of 'giving up' situations into the hands of God and also provides a dramatic visual aid.
- Hold out situations to God while lying on the floor.
- Commit ourselves to:
  pray for the situation itself;
  act to change it;
  tell others of the situation.
- Declaration to prayer: we don't have to mumble our prayers, we can shout them to God as a declaration to him and to one another.

BIBLE INVESTIGATION

Divide the whole group into threes, and give each small group one of the following passages and a set of questions to investigate.

Exodus 3: 7–10
Hebrews 13:3
Mark 8:31
1 Peter 2: 21–24
1 Peter 4: 12–19

Ask the small groups to consider the following questions.

- What is God's reaction to suffering?
- What should our attitude be towards those who are suffering?
- What suffering should we expect, if any, in our lives?

EXTRA ACTIVITIES

WHO AM I?

This could be used as a warm-up session.

Pass out a postcard-sized piece of paper to each person.

Each person writes on the paper four things about themselves. These could include:

- One thing about their appearance
- One thing about their character
- One unknown fact about their history
- One hope they have for the future

Collect all the papers together in a bin or a polythene bag.

Invite volunteers to come out to the front, take a piece of paper and read it to the rest of the group. Everyone else is to try and guess who is being described.

Before the exercise becomes boring, stop. Ask the group to get into threes and come up with suggestions as to why it was easy or difficult to identify group members from the facts which had been disclosed.

Allow each group one minute to report back its findings.

CRAZY GOD QUIZ

Give every member of the group a questionnaire like the following. This is in the form of a star profile as found in any teen magazine. For the GOD FILE: young people need to imagine who God's favourite band would be, what his favourite food would be, etc . . . The results will vary depending on age and culture but their choices will always say something about how they view God, no matter how silly they might seem at the time.

CRAZY GOD QUIZ

THE GOD FILE

If I had to give God
a colour, it would be.................................. Fave band

Why?..

What God likes
best about me is .... Fave food

Why?..

My favourite
bit of God's Book is.................................... Best moment

....

God influences
how much of my life???............................. Person most pleased He
created

 0%   5%   10%   20%   30%   40%

50%   60%   70%   80%   90%   100%

(circle the nearest answer)

God makes me feel.................................... Most likely to say

Least likely to say

One question I have always wanted to ask God is:

....

....

VIDEO PSALM

Many of the Psalms give us verbal pictures reflecting the world and views of God.

In your group, create your own psalm to reflect your own culture, lifestyle and experiences. Use a video camera, words, music, etc. BUT: make it no longer than three minutes.

It could be a psalm of praise, of thanksgiving, of repentance, sorrow, creation, beauty, etc . . . the possibilities are as endless as your imagination.

Read a few of David's Psalms if you are short on ideas.

MODULE TWO

Jesus
INTRODUCTION

This module will look at Jesus and in so doing will explore the core of the Christian faith.

We believe in one Lord Jesus Christ, the only son of God eternally begotten from the Father

1. Jesus was fully God, fully man: two natures, one person. We need to be careful in our teaching not to give the impression either that Jesus was just a good man like us (only better), or that he was God but he was just pretending to be human.

2. Jesus lived a sinless life. Although, because of his human nature, Jesus would have been tempted to sin in much the same way as we all are, he was different in that he never did sin.

3. Jesus' teaching was radical in content and form. Jesus shocked the religious authorities of his day, confused and frustrated the so-called 'godly' people but gave liberation to all those who truly heard his message. His message and person still have the same power today.

4. Jesus performed miracles. When Jesus was around, things happened. People were healed and set free.

5. Jesus died and then rose from the dead. If Jesus is not risen then our faith is a delusion. The resurrection is the crux of our faith and it is important that our young people realize that all their faith hinges on this important fact.

Session 1
THE JESUS EFFECT

AIM

To look at the effects of Jesus' death and resurrection.

WARM-UPS

Use one or two of the following to demonstrate the starting point: that effects have causes.

Interviews with elderly people

Arrange for two of your junior leaders or older members to visit a number of elderly people (perhaps those known in the congregation or through contacts) with a tape recorder or video. Ask them to talk about the effects of a major event in their lives (getting married, the war, their first child, becoming a Christian, etc) without mentioning what the event itself actually was.

Record half a dozen or so of these and play them to the youth group, who have to try and identify what each event is.

Mystery tasks

One at a time, perhaps at the beginning of the session, volunteers are sent to another room to perform a mystery task lasting perhaps only ninety seconds. When they return, the remainder of the group have to guess what the mystery task was without asking questions as to its nature.

Mystery tasks could include:

- Cycling half a mile on an exercise bike.
- Chopping up three peeled onions, finely.
- Retrieving ten Smarties from a bowl of flour with only teeth (. . . and not wiping face afterwards!).

- Listening to music.
- Bobbing for five apples, from water, syrup, flour, etc.

Inventions

Divide the group into teams of three and give each team a MYSTERY EFFECTS sheet. The teams have to try and identify the inventor and the invention referred to, and its effects for us today. The first team to do so is the winner, otherwise the team to get the most answers correct in a given time wins.

MYSTERY EFFECTS

Who are each of the inventors, what did they invent and what are the effects for today?

1. Born in 1879, he died in 1955.
This is one invention that has only been used twice.

2. Nikolaus Otto's 1876 invention used by two Germans, Karl and Gottlieb.

3. Why did a Scotsman say *'Come here, Watson, I need you'*?

4. On 17 December 1903, two brothers, Wilbur and Orville, did something at Kitty Hawk.

5. This Italian (1874–1937) reached across the channel in 1899.

Answers

1. *Atomic bomb* Albert Einstein
2. *Four-stroke engine* Daimler & Benz
3. *Telephone* Alexander Bell
4. *Manned flight* Wright Brothers
5. *Radio message* Marconi

WORD-UP

One way in which we can understand the significance of an event is to look at it in the light of history. Here we are going to look at the effects of Jesus' life ten to thirty years after his death.

ACTION

Divide the group into small groups (perhaps three or four, depending on the size of your group).

Pass out to each of the small groups one of the cards below. (You may need several copies of each for there to be enough.)

SOMETHING WORTH SUFFERING FOR

1 Peter 1: 3–9; 2 Timothy 4: 1–8; 2 Timothy 2: 8–13; Philippians 1: 21; 2 Corinthians 11: 23–31

1. What did the writers believe that Jesus had achieved?
2. How did they describe and demonstrate this?
3. How do they challenge us today?

SOMETHING PROMISES ETERNAL LIFE

Titus 3: 4–7; Philippians 3: 7–11; 1 Corinthians 15: 20–23

1. What did the writers believe that Jesus had achieved?
2. How did they describe and demonstrate this?
3. How does this challenge us today?

SOMETHING SETS US FREE FROM SIN

Hebrews 10: 19–24; 1 Peter 3: 15–22; 1 John 1: 5–9; 1 John 4: 14–16; Romans 6: 1–14

1. What did the writers believe that Jesus had achieved?
2. How did they describe and demonstrate this?
3. How do they challenge us today?

SOMETHING CHANGES OUR LIFESTYLE

Colossians 3: 1–11; Philippians 2: 1–5; Ephesians 5: 1–8

1. What did the writers believe that Jesus had achieved?
2. How did they describe and demonstrate this?
3. How do they challenge us today?

SOUND BACK

After fifteen to twenty minutes allow one representative from each group a couple of minutes to share some of their thoughts and findings with the whole group.

When all the groups have reported back and you have taken up any points or questions that have arisen which you feel appropriate to pursue, use the following (again, if you feel it to be appropriate).

CLOSING WORSHIP

Prepare some of the young people in advance for this so that they each have a candle and a card detailing facts about an early Christian, which they will read out. The group sits in a circle around a central candle or focus. Quietly sing an appropriate worship song. Those with candles light them.

Leader: The Early Christians believed Jesus:
* was worth suffering for
* sets us free from sin
* promises us eternal life
* changes our life and our relationships

Members: [Read from their cards and blow out their candles as they finish. (This needs to be done slowly and with dignity to be effective.)]

PAUL
Paul persecuted Christians until his conversion. He endured gruelling miss-ions and founded many churches. He was beheaded for his faith in AD 64.

JAMES
James was the younger brother of Jesus. He led the Early Church in Jerusalem. He died for his faith in AD 62.

JAMES

James was the brother of John, a fisherman who followed Jesus.

He was beheaded for his faith eleven years after the Resurrection.

PETER

Peter was the rock upon which Jesus said his Church would be built.

He was crucified in Rome in AD 64.

BARTHOLOMEW

Bartholomew followed Jesus and was anointed by the Holy Spirit as a Missionary.

He was whipped to death in Armenia.

BARNABAS

Barnabas was Paul's companion.
He was the son of Encouragement, used mightily by God.
He was martyred at Salamis in AD 61.

Session 2
JESUS AND HIS TEACHING

AIM

To explore the content and message of Jesus' teaching.

WARM-UPS

There is no short-cut to looking at the teaching of Jesus. We need to be reading the Bible and constantly trying to apply it to our own lives. Here are three warm-ups to help you identify how much your young people already know and some of the issues that are especially relevant to them.

True or False?

Ask the following questions and get everyone to indicate whether they think they are true or false. The answers are indicated after each question.

1. Jesus was white, European (*False*)
2. Jesus taught people about a new religion (*False*)
3. Jesus taught about God's Kingdom (*True*)
4. Jesus taught that looking lustfully at a woman is the same as committing adultery (*True*)
5. Jesus taught about ten virgins (*True*)
6. Jesus said that he had come to bring division: father against son and mother against daughter etc (*True*)
7. Jesus taught us to fight our enemies (*False*)
8. Jesus said that whoever is not against us is for us (*True*)
9. Jesus taught that listening to God is more important than washing up (*True*)
10. Jesus taught that the Kingdom of God was at hand (*True*)

Mastermind challenge

Use the same or similar questions to those above and set up the equivalent of a mastermind challenge, using individuals or small teams in the spotlight.

After hours

A warm-up specifically aimed at older groups. Select four or five members to play out the roles on a late-night chat show for which the topic is 'The teaching of Jesus'.

Characters could include:

- A doubting bishop
- A Christian sports personality
- An agony aunt
- A journalist

Give the participants time to prepare their characters. On the evening, set the scene as best you can with any props you can lay your hands on. Allow ten or fifteen minutes for the 'show' to run, depending on how it is going.

MAIN SESSION

WORD-UP

The way in which we can discover more about what Jesus taught is by studying what he said and looking at how the apostles began to apply this teaching. The four Gospels contain most of this teaching material and we see its later applications in Acts.

Divide into smaller groups to look at some of the themes of Jesus' teaching in the Gospel material. Each group is to read their chapters and see what they can dig out on their theme. There are three themes: the Kingdom, love and life-style.

The Kingdom: Read Matthew 13–18. What did Jesus teach on
   the Kingdom of God or Heaven?
Love: Read Luke 14–20. What did Jesus say about love?
Life-style: Read Luke 6–13. What did Jesus teach about how we
   should live?

If there were any aspects of Jesus' teaching discovered in the session above which people found especially difficult, read out the relevant piece of Scripture and open the passage up to the floor. Perhaps you could offer a mid-week Bible study in the future on the issue that caused the difficulty, or arrange for someone to come in and speak on the issue.

OPEN FLOOR

Have a general discussion based on the following questions.

• What do you think would have been the reaction of
   today's society or Church to Jesus' teaching if he had come
   to our time instead of first-century Palestine?
• Have people learnt anything particular this evening about
   what Jesus said? Something that surprised, shocked or
   encouraged them?

Life-style

INTRODUCTION

'Christian faith is really easy just as long as it doesn't make any difference to me', or to put the same sentiment a different way: to know whether Jesus is Lord in our lives, we must see what we do when we want something and God says no, or when he is telling us to do something that we don't want to do.

If the demands of the Gospel are identical to what our young people want to do anyway then life-style is an area where some 'injected' challenges would be good.

Life-style is how we express our faith day by day. I'm always amazed at the list of professions and jobs which first-century Christians could not do because they were seen to be incompatible with their Christian faith. These days we sometimes go to great lengths (and even change churches) to justify virtually any life-style as a Christian.

This module looks at some of the areas where a young person's life-style and that of their peers can be at variance with their faith. It works through a number of issues:

1. Is eating a sin?
2. TV and video
3. Stress
4. Life-style audit
5. Making moral choices
6. Vegetarianism

Session 4 is a 'life-style audit', and this gives an opportunity for the young people to make a personal response to the challenge of a Christian life-style.

Session 1
IS EATING A SIN?

Sometimes it feels, if we are to believe everything that the media tell us, that everything we eat is bad for us. Use this session to try and look beyond the messages we are given about food by the media and concentrate on what God says about the issue.

AIM

To look at what and when we eat.

WARM-UPS

Choose one of these warm-ups to get the group thinking about some of the issues prior to doing the main session.

The snitch quiz

Pass out to everyone a copy of the quiz.

Answers

1b, 2d, 3b, 4c, 5d: You are a chocoholic with a sweet tooth.
1d, 2a, 3c, 4b, 5b: PIG!
1c, 2c, 3d, 4d, 5a: You worry about your weight and what you
        eat.
1a, 2b, 3a, 4a, 5c: Sensible and normal.

Food brainstorm

Record parts of a few TV adverts for food products or show parts of food adverts to the group. Have the group guess the product. Do a group brainstorm of as many food products advertised on the television as they can think of, make a list and put it up on the wall.

Break down into small groups and discuss:

1. How are the advertisers trying to sell their product? What techniques are they using?
2. Who is the advert designed to appeal to?

THE SNITCH QUIZ

1. You are sitting in front of a video, on your own for the evening. *Would you:*

   (a) Nibble a biscuit or two
   (b) Hit the popcorn or chocolate
   (c) Eat nothing
   (d) Wipe out a plateful of whatever is in the kitchen

2. You are in town with friends and it is nearly lunchtime. *Would you:*

   (a) Go to a fast food place for lunch
   (b) Pick up a cake or pasty from the baker's
   (c) Say your Mum's doing lunch when you get home
   (d) Get a 400g chocbar to share

3. You are involved in a twenty-four-hour fast to raise funds for the Third World. *Would you:*

   (a) Eat normally just before and fast for the whole period
   (b) Try hard, but succumb to the odd chocolate bar
   (c) Pig out before it starts and the second it ends
   (d) Take extra exercise to increase the effect

4. You are eating out in a restaurant with your family. *Would you:*

   (a) Choose small portions of exotic and different things
   (b) Go for what you know and plenty of it
   (c) Miss the starter to make sure you've room for pudding
   (d) Have just a starter and say you are not hungry

5. You have only got an hour to get ready to go out for the evening. You've not eaten since breakfast. *Would you:*

   (a) Forget food as it takes an hour to get ready
   (b) Cook something to eat and forget about getting ready
   (c) Grab a quick snack
   (d) Take the biscuit tin upstairs and demolish the contents while getting ready

3. We all have to eat: why are the advertisers marketing their product in this way?

Tasting

Organize your own food-tasting session using different products: digestive biscuits, colas or similar products. Try the brand name against the supermarket's own brand.

Label the cups, plates, etc, with letters, so you know which is which. Everyone doing the tasting gives the product a mark out of ten for quality as you determine. Add up the totals on a flip chart alongside the relevant letters and then reveal which product was which.

Break down into small groups and discuss:

1. Were you surprised at the results?
2. How important are the differences between the products?
3. When would any of these differences become irrelevant?

MAIN SESSION
DEBATE

- Food is an idol *or*
- Supermarkets are the worship centres of the community *or*
- The youth group believes that we should eat to live not live to eat

A couple of weeks before the session, choose people to speak for or against the motion. This means they can prepare their speeches. Give them help where necessary.

DISCUSSION CARDS

Members draw Discussion Cards for the whole group or small groups to talk about. Suggestions for cards might be as below.

1. Who gains from food fads and scares?
2. To be fat is a sin in today's society.
3. Women are more valuable to food advertising strategies than men.
4. External appearance is over-important today.

5. Westerners eat too much.
6. The fun has been taken out of food.

GOING FURTHER – BIBLE STUDY

Hand out cards as below to small groups or one to the whole group.

---

1. FOOD AND THE LAW
Read Deuteronomy 4: 3–21

- Why did God give these instructions to his people?
- What would they demonstrate to other tribes and nations?
- What principles could we apply from this passage today?

---

2. FOOD AND GREED
Read Amos 4: 1, 5: 11–13, 8: 1–6

- What is God concerned with about food in these passages?
- Food seems to be symbolic of wider problems. What might these problems be?

---

3. FOOD AND NEED
Read Matthew 6: 25–34

- What are God's concerns in this passage?
- If we are to seek the Kingdom first, what does that mean about what we eat and drink?
- In what ways can we apply this today?

---

4. FOOD AND FREEDOM
Read Matthew 15: 1–20

- What was Jesus saying about food in this passage?
- What important truths are contained in this?
- What are the implications for us today?

ACTION

What can I do?

Plan together some practical ways to put God's guidelines on food into practice. Discuss how young people today might respond to the media bombardment and associated guilt which are connected with what we eat and drink.

TELEVISION AND VIDEO

AIM

To look at the content and influence of TV and videos.

MAIN SESSION VIDEO VIEW

Draw up a list of the Top Ten videos for the preceding month (a list of these can be obtained from free magazines given out in video hire shops or is often found in local newspapers). Pass out the score sheet as below.

Name of video	Story line	Content	Positive Christian influence	Sex	Violence	Total
1						
2						
3						
4						
5						
6						
7						
8						
9						
10						

Ask members of the group to complete the sheet *only* for the videos that they have *seen*, and to give a mark out of ten for each of the categories.

Category key

Give the group the following guidelines to help them fill in the form.

Content How is the material of the video presented? Are there different ideas being put forward?

Is the music throughout the video suitable? And so on.

Score 10 if the content is good and score 1 if the content is worse than bad. (This score should reflect the artistic merit of the film, not specifically its Christian content.)

Positive Christian influence Does this film uphold and support Christian values?

Is the video supporting values which are neutral or ones that undermine Christian ethics?

Score 10 for strongly upholds Christian values and 1 if it undermines.

Sex Is there promiscuous or adulterous sex portrayed in the video? Is this material over-explicit or unnecessary? Score 10 if the film conveys Christian stands and graduate the score down to 1 if the portrayal is unnecessarily graphic.

Violence What kind of violence is contained in the film? Is it essential to enhance the story or is it put in just for effect?

Score 10 if there is no violence at all and 1 if it is gratuitous and unnecessary.

Total Add all the scores to find the total score for each video on the list. The higher the score the better the film.

REPORT BACK

Talk about the scores for each film given by different members of the group. Do this as a whole group, with members who wish to share their totals, or have small groups discuss their totals and compile group totals.

Session 3
STRESS

AIM

To investigate stress.

EQUIPMENT AND PREPARATION

Gather the ingredients needed for the warm-up activities.

WARM-UP

Play a number of games which have a high stress element.

Jenga

This is a game where players have to remove blocks from a wooden tower without knocking it down, and then use those pieces removed to make the original tower taller.

Card towers

Have one pack of cards per team. The task is to build the highest card tower (with all members of the team playing a part in the construction) in three minutes.

Paired stretch elastic bands

Divide the group into pairs and give each couple a large elastic band. The competition is to see how far each couple can stretch their elastic band between them without it breaking. A game of nerve and stupidity!

MAIN SESSION

Pass out a STRESS TESTER SHEET to each person.

STRESS TESTER SHEET

HOW STRESSED ARE YOU?

WHICH OF THE FOLLOWING HAVE YOU EXPERIENCED
OVER THE LAST WEEK?

	Yes	No
PHYSICAL		
Do you find sleeping at night difficult?		
Do you want to sleep all day?		
Do you have frequent headaches?		
Are there times when your stomach churns or is in knots?		
RELATIONSHIPS		
Are there people who you avoid meeting or spending time with?		
Is your relationship with your parents worse than usual?		
Do you get on less well with your friends?		
Do you find it more difficult to pray or read your Bible?		
BEHAVIOURAL		
Are you watching more TV or videos alone to get away?		
Are you having dreams or nightmares?		
Do you find yourself losing your temper more often?		
Do your favourite activities, hobbies or foods hold less interest?		

After everyone has completed their Stress Sheet, share answers.

WORD-UP

Stress can be caused by a variety of things. One of these things for us as Christians might be that our 'insides' don't match up with our 'outsides'. We will be looking a little at this next, but basically this is when our actions do not match up with how we are really feeling inside.

INSTANT DRAMAS

Divide the group into teams of three people. Each team has about three minutes to produce a spontaneous and instant dramatic sketch (not a masterpiece) on a situation that will illustrate this problem of our 'outsides not matching up with our insides' in the Christian life.

After five minutes show the dramas.

Here are some hints as to ideas to put into these situations.

Outside characteristics	*Inside realities*
Boasting	Fear of failure
Lying	Fear of rejection
Super spiritual	Worried by exams
Always over-helpful	Worried about boyfriend or girlfriend
Crowd pleasing	Not having a boyfriend or girlfriend
Troublemaker	Worried about parents
Boasts about Bible study	Scared of . . .
Always making fun of others	Struggling with faith
	Low self-worth

ADVICE SHOP

Talk in the large group about what they think people should have done in their drama situations if it were real life. How can these characters match their insides with their outsides?

STEP ONE	QUESTIONS
1 KINGS 19: 11–13	1. Who should we talk to when stressed, and how?
PSALM 46: 10	2. How does God react when we're stressed?
PHILIPPIANS 4: 6	3. How easy is it for you to pray when you are stressed?

STEP TWO	QUESTIONS
GALATIANS 6: 2	1. Who should we talk to when we are stressed, and how?
PROVERBS 12: 15	2. How do we react if we don't hear what we want to hear?
PROVERBS 12: 26	3. Do you find it easier to share your problems or have others share theirs?

STEP THREE	QUESTIONS
1 KINGS 19: 3–9	1. What needs was God concerned about?
	2. What was the result of ignoring these needs for Elijah?
	3. What areas of our 'needs' go when we are stressed?

STEP FOUR	QUESTIONS
MATTHEW 6: 25–27	1. What does God say about our anxieties and cares?
1 PETER 5: 7	2. What good does concentrating on them do?
	3. Which areas that we can do nothing about, stress us out?

CONCLUSION

When all the groups are finished, have them report back to the whole group. It might be worth leading the discussion to point out:

STEP 1 TALK AND LISTEN TO GOD

STEP 2 TALK AND LISTEN TO FRIENDS

STEP 3 CHECK YOUR CIRCUMSTANCES

STEP 4 RECOGNIZE THERE ARE SOME THINGS YOU CAN DO NOTHING ABOUT

BIBLE INVESTIGATION

Pass out INVESTIGATION CARDS either to pairs or to small groups. If the groups manage to finish inside the time they can swap cards with another group.

So the four steps to reduce stress are:

1. Talk to God
2. Talk to friends
3. Balance your body (we all need sleep, food, exercise . . .)
4. Forget the things you cannot do anything about

Then use some relaxing music, quiet choruses or similar on tape and spend a few minutes as a group listening to the music and giving any burdens to God.

Session 4
LIFE-STYLE AUDIT

AIM

This session was originally intended as a conclusion to the whole Teaching Module on Life-style, after looking at some of the issues affecting how we live as Christians in a non-Christian society. The AUDIT SHEET helps us to draw lots of thoughts and issues together in our minds as we look at some of the areas of our lives which we can change. The COMMITMENT CARD is a way of cementing the young people's discoveries about their lives.

The life-style audit can also be used in conjunction with the Bible investigation as a more general session using the audit sheet as a way into looking at our lives and the commitment card again as a pledge to try and change something small.

PREPARATION

Photocopy the Audit Sheet and the Commitment Cards. (See diagram.)

LIFESTYLE AUDIT SHEET

YOUR TIME

1. Fill in the two time charts on how you use your time:

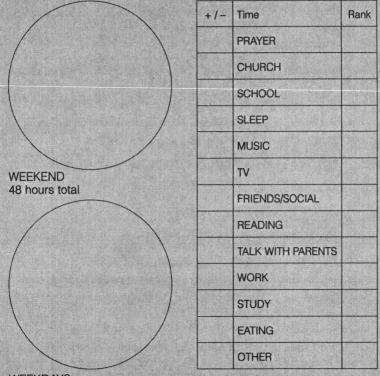

WEEKEND
48 hours total

WEEKDAYS
120 hours total

+ / –	Time	Rank
	PRAYER	
	CHURCH	
	SCHOOL	
	SLEEP	
	MUSIC	
	TV	
	FRIENDS/SOCIAL	
	READING	
	TALK WITH PARENTS	
	WORK	
	STUDY	
	EATING	
	OTHER	

* Next to each of the time uses above, put a rank number for how important this use is to you. i.e. 13 = least important and 1 = most important.

* QUESTION: How does this ranking compare with how you use your time?

(If something is really important to you, are you spending enough or too much time doing it? Put a (+) next to anything you feel you need to spend more time on and a (–) next to anything you feel you should spend less time on.)

YOUR MONEY

Where does your money come from and where does it go?

INCOME £ $ EXPENDITURE £ $

Source	Monthly Amount		Monthly Amount	+ or −
		Fast food		
1)		Clothes		
		Music		
2)		Sweets		
		Alcohol/fags		
3)		Rent/board		
		God		
TOTAL		Hobbies		
		Savings		
		Entertainment		
		Other		
		Other		
		TOTAL		

Look at how you spend your money.

Does the above reflect what you feel is important?

Put a (+) next to those things you feel you ought to be spending more money on and a (−) next to those you feel you ought to spend less on.

YOUR MIND

What do I feed my mind on? How important are the following?

Mind-food	Priority	Time spent (per week)	+or –
TV			
Videos			
Magazine			
Friends' views			
Teachers			
Youth leader			
Minister			
Bible			
Newspapers			
Books			
Parents			
Other			

Q. Look at what you think influences you most. How does this seem when you look at the things you spend most of your time on?

Put a (+) next to the things you think, in view of your priorities, that you should spend more time being influenced by and a (–) next to the things you reckon you should let yourself be influenced less by.

MAIN SESSION

Hand out audit sheets to everyone. These are to be confidential to each group member and you must assure them that this will be so. Allow enough time so that everyone can fill in their sheets.

While the sheets are being completed, allow people to ask any questions which they might have, making sure that everyone knows that there will be opportunities later on that evening to discuss things which they have felt challenged by.

The Audit Sheets are to be kept by the individuals themselves.

WORD-UP

Being a Christian is not just about assenting to a set of philosophical positions but about a personal relationship with God, following him through Jesus with a new set of priorities for our lifestyle.

BIBLE INVESTIGATION

Divide into small groups. Each group should read one of the following parables and then answer the questions.

Matthew 25: 31–46
Matthew 20: 1–16
Matthew 18: 23–34
Luke 12: 42–48

- What demands do the implications of the parable put on our life-style in terms of how we use our time, our money, our gifts and our opportunities.
- How do these demands compare with our own personal priorities as shown on our Audit Sheets?

CONCLUSION

Ask members (if they want to) to fill in 'for their eyes only' one of the commitment cards to remind them of the challenge they felt regarding certain areas of their life-style. These cards are, as with the audit sheet, confidential, but say that you will be available if people want to talk or pray about anything.

Close in prayer.

LIFE-STYLE COMMITMENT

I *(write your name here)*_____ am committed to God's Kingdom and to his people in that Kingdom.

This commitment has an impact on every bit of my life: how I spend my time and my money, how I feed my body and my mind, how I use the resources of this world and the gifts which God has given me.

My priorities for change are:

1 _____

2 _____

3 _____

4 _____

Signed_____

MAKING MORAL CHOICES

AIM

To look at how we make moral and personal choices and decisions as Christians.

PREPARATION AND EQUIPMENT

You will need to draw and label shapes as shown on p. 134. Use card rather than paper. Prepare enough card copies of the Moral Triangle so that everyone can have one each. Gather enough scissors so that everyone can have a pair each. You will also need a large sheet of paper or overhead projector and pens for the brainstorm warm-up.

WARM-UP

Play one or both of the following warm-up games.

God wants versus my wants

Brainstorm some of the moral choices that members expect to have to make or be faced with over the next few years. After all these have been written up on a large sheet of paper, characterize each choice by marking them with one of the following:

G = God wants   M =My wants

Scruples

Borrow a game of Scruples from somewhere and play it for about twenty minutes: a fun way to expose people to immediate moral choice-making.

MAIN SESSION

Pass out a pair of scissors and a copy of the Moral Triangle to everyone and explain that you are going to suggest some guidelines for making moral decisions – some that are true and

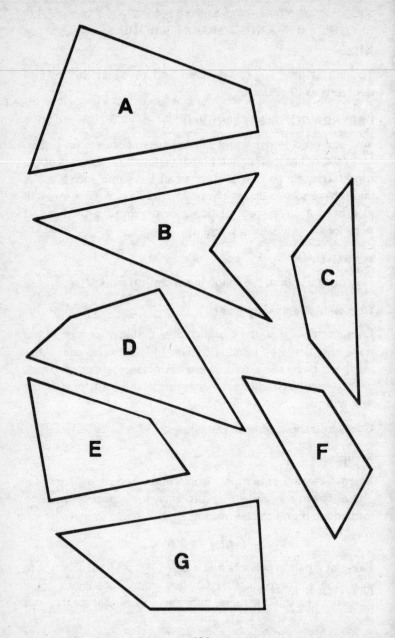

some that are obviously false. Each guideline will have a letter to describe it – A to G, corresponding with the shapes you have drawn.

When each guideline is read out, if members think that it is a Christian way of making a decision they are to cut out the corresponding piece of the Moral Triangle. If, at the end of the game, they have guessed correctly all the Christian guidelines, they should be able to compile an equilateral triangle from the pieces they have cut out.

GUIDELINES

Guideline A: Pray, asking God to guide you in your prayers.

Guideline B: Look at your situation and your circumstances and see whether God is opening or closing doors for you through them.

Guideline C: Lay out a deal – if God does 'x' then you will know that 'y' is what he wants you to do.

Guideline D: Look at the Bible – in the light of God's call on your life, is the action you are considering compatible?

Guideline E: Look at the Bible – in the light of what God is like, is the action you are contemplating what God would want you to do?

Guideline F: Ask older Christians and leaders for their advice and guidance.

Guideline G: Check out what you are feeling: does this feel right in your heart?

Allow members a couple of minutes to assemble their triangles. Options (C) and (G) are false ways in themselves to seek God's guidance.

WORD-UP

Explain that feelings are very changeable as a basis for making decisions. Twisting God's arm or randomly opening our Bibles are a long way short of developing the long-lasting relationship that God is longing to have with all of us. Part of the process of building that relationship is getting to know God and discerning what his will is. Gradually we become more and more aware of what kinds of action are compatible.

GOING FURTHER

In pairs, choose two or three of the issues that were brainstormed at the beginning of the session and that were characterized with an 'M'. Consider them in the light of the Guidelines A, B, D, E and F.

Session 6
VEGETARIANISM

A recent survey showed that about 28,000 people become vegetarians in the UK each day; four and a half million people do not eat red meat and two in every five people have considered becoming vegetarian. Is this a passing phase that Christians can ignore or is it an issue we need to address biblically?

WARM-UP

if there are any vegetarians in the youth group, ask them to cook some vegetarian food for people to taste. (You should reimburse their costs.) Food is a great way to start a youth group evening and many vegetarians will love the excuse to 'show their wares'.

MAIN SESSION

Divide the group into three teams and allocate each a different area to investigate. You could have the questions for each team on a card. This is an exercise that is probably best done over a couple of weeks, so tell everyone that they will be asked to report back in two weeks' time.

1. *The cruelty angle*

How do we treat animals: how are they kept, transported, killed?

What does the Bible tell us about animals and our responsibility towards them?

2. *The Third World angle*

What is the impact of our life-style on people elsewhere?

Do Third World cash crops end up feeding animals here so we can eat meat instead of feeding people in the countries where they are grown?

What does the Bible tell us about our responsibility to the poor and oppressed and what does it say about exploitation?

3. *The personal angle*

Vegetarianism: Is it first a question of taste and preference or is it a health issue?

What does the Bible tell us about looking after ourselves?

Explain to each of the groups that they have two weeks before they will have to report back to the whole group on their area of investigation and biblical reflection.

When the two weeks are up, ask the three teams to present their findings in ways that they feel are appropriate and hold a discussion where groups can share their feelings about what they and the other groups discovered.

GOING FURTHER: PART 1

Divide the group into pairs. Read the passages. Each pair should read Daniel 1: 1–20, Acts 10: 9–19 and Romans 14: 1–3.

One person in each pair is to argue in support of vegetarianism using the passage from Daniel, and the other person in each pair is to argue against vegetarianism using the other passages.

Allow ten minutes for preparation, and then have a discussion using only the biblical material.

GOING FURTHER: PART 2

How does the biblical material compare with the findings that the three research groups made?

Have your views about vegetarianism changed since starting this study?

Will you be changing what you eat either to or from vegetarianism after discussing this information?

Spiritual growth
INTRODUCTION

We have an aim in our church youth work. It is not a very original one: Paul talks about it and I have a feeling that God has been saying a little bit about it for a while.

What is it? It is: 'To see young people grow towards maturity in Christ.'

For young people (indeed, for everyone), spiritual growth is not a smooth, steady curve upwards. It is more akin to the latest Roller Coaster at Alton Towers: you go up, you go down, you stand on your head and through your stomach to end up exactly where you started. I'm perfectly sure that the reason behind my not really being keen on those kind of rides is that they remind me too vividly of my job! Anyway, this spiritual growth needs gentle encouragement and nurturing. Our young people need the boost of knowing that they are not quite back at the point at which they began and have made some measure of progress.

We also need to prepare them for the tough times. One of the reasons that 50 per cent of teenagers drop out of church life is exactly this: we haven't, in the past, prepared them for when the times get tough. If we are telling our young people to 'come to Jesus and everything will be OK', when everything suddenly is not OK they will turn back to us and say that it is all not true and our credibility has been smashed. These young people are some of the toughest nuts to crack in our youth work today – those who say they have tried God and it 'did not work'.

We need to prepare our young people for the spiritual battles, developing their tools for spiritual growth, ensuring their expectations are biblical and realistic and giving them the resources to survive the hard times. All this is not easy and not something that can be achieved in three sessions: we need to back up our teaching with our time, openness, honesty, faith, prayer and our whole lives.

Session 1
FACING THE CHALLENGE OF GROWTH

AIM

Growing as a Christian can be compared with climbing a rock face: sometimes we can see where we are going and make steady progress, but at other times it feels as if we're holding on by our fingernails only. This session provides an opportunity for us to look at key stages in our spiritual journeys and to examine the times when we have grown.

PREPARATION AND EQUIPMENT

Paper and pens. Climbing equipment (if you're game for the warm-up!), overhead projector or photocopies of instructions for Main Session.

WARM-UP

Street scaling

If yours is a group willing to try daft things (well, at least once anyway!) then this is the ultimate for you: borrow some climbing equipment, get all dressed up to climb and do a horizontal climb across the church, up the high street, etc.

The knack is all in the acting: be real. Use all the aids you can to scale the high street: attach your rope to lamp posts, telephone boxes, pillar boxes, etc . . . put your base camp at the bottom of the high street and your youth group flag at the top.

Have two competing teams (if you can find enough brave enough to meet the challenge). The most realistic team wins.

MAIN SESSION

Spiritual climbs

This is another way of looking at our spiritual journeys. See the instructions below.

Pass out pens and paper to everyone, and put the instructions for constructing Spiritual climbs plus an example onto the overhead projector or flip chart, or give everyone a photocopy. It can be a great encouragement to the group to draw your own climb as the example. If you are honest, this will encourage them to be honest too, and it will also make the exercise easier to understand.

When everyone has constructed their spiritual climb, divide into groups of four or five and ask each person to share from their chart.

INSTRUCTIONS

Draw a cliff face which represents your spiritual journey. It may help you to think about:
1. Where was the going hard or smooth?
2. What were the overhangs you struggled with?
3. Where did you fall off and who pulled you back?
4. Who climbed with you at different stages?
5. What were the key moments in your climb: the pitons which secured your rope to the cliff face?

When everyone has shared their cliff faces with their group, brainstorm in small groups the things that caused people to fall off the cliff face, the overhangs that caused people to struggle and the pitons which secured their rope.

SOUND BACK

Each small group reads its list and a list for the whole group is compiled onto the overhead projector or flip chart. Talk about how the group as a whole can help people to grow spiritually. Discuss the following questions:

- How can we maximize the secure points in our group and in people's lives?
- Who has fallen off the cliff totally from this group and what can we do about it? How can we stop it from happening to others?

GOING FURTHER

The goal of our spiritual journey is to be more Christ-like. We need to dig into our Bibles to find out how we can do this.

BIBLE INVESTIGATION

Ask everyone in the group to read:

2 Corinthians 3: 18
Philippians 3: 12–17
Philippians 2: 1–8
Colossians 1: 10

Each of these verses teaches us important facts about spiritual growth.

- What are they?
- How do we apply these to our own group and personal lives?

Session 2
WALKING WITH GOD

AIM

To compare the internal reality of a relationship with God with the external expressions of faith.

WARM-UP

Pass out a variety of Christian tracts, leaflets, etc, on becoming a Christian. Brainstorm onto a flip chart or overhead projector the internal realities of becoming a Christian as against the external ones. For instance, an internal reality might be a love of God; an external reality might be a desire to worship; an internal reality is usually something that challenges us; an external reality is usually a sign of an internal reality.

WORD-UP

We often talk about the externals of the Christian faith and use them to measure how well we think we are doing in our Christian life: in our Bible study, in prayer, in sharing our faith, in church attendance, in giving money and time ... but what's happening inside?

BIBLE INVESTIGATION

As a group read Matthew 23: 23–28.

Jesus clearly warns us that it is not just the external things that have to change, both at our conversion and throughout our lives, but also the things which are inside us.

Break into smaller study groups. Use the passages below to discover some of the internal things that might need to change as we grow in faith. Divide the passages amongst the groups.

1 Peter 3: 14–18	James 1: 19–21	Matthew 5: 21–24
Matthew 5: 22–28	Romans 12: 3–8	Galatians 6: 22–26

List the characteristics found in the passages on a flip chart or overhead projector as the groups report back.

Ask everyone in the group to go round and share spontaneously what they think might be the three most important things to God on the list.

Which three things are the most important for us as individuals? (Do not share these out loud, but spend a few moments quietly praying about them.)

WORD-UP

Use the passages below to illustrate a short talk or use the passages and statements as a basis for group discussion.

Theme: How can we keep our internals in order?

1. Keep short accounts with God

'Don't let the sun go down . . .' (Ephesians 4: 26.)
We should make sure that we forgive others quickly and seek forgiveness from God every day. Rubbish is easier to put out for the dustmen if it is in small bags.

2. Keep shared accounts

'Bear one another's burdens . . .' (Galatians 6: 1–2.)
God wants us to get together with other Christians to share our troubles and problems and to care for each other. If we are in a group and we start to drift, the others will gently guide us back.

3. Be under account

'Obey your leaders and submit to those in authority.' (Hebrews 13: 17.)
When we submit ourselves to our leaders and are not acting rebelliously we are more likely to develop the right witness and healthy relationships in the Church, and to have the support we need.

4. Keep an open account

'Men loved darkness rather than light, because their deeds were evil.' (John 3:19.)
To ensure that there are no hidden areas of our lives, we need to be open to God and open to others.

CONCLUSION

End the session with a time of prayer when people can commit their walk with God.

Session 3
WHEN THE GOING GETS TOUGH

AIM

To look at some of our fears and misconceptions when the Christian faith seems to be very hard going.

PREPARATION

Draw up and position (as below) a number of road signs and their explanations round the room.

WARM-UP

Brainstorm what the members find tough about the Christian life onto an overhead projector or flip chart. After the list has been completed, ask the group to look at the road signs and the comments you have placed round the room.

SING IT AGAIN –
EVERYTHING WILL
BE ALL RIGHT.

YOU CAN'T BE
A REAL CHRISTIAN
IF YOU DOUBT

THIS TIME YOU'VE
BLOWN IT –
NO RETURN FROM HERE

EVERYONE ELSE
IS DOING OK –
GOING THE OTHER WAY

IF ONLY I HAD
MORE FAITH

YOU CAN'T ESCAPE
PAST SINS

When everyone has had the opportunity to look around at the road signs ask them which of the road signs were familiar to their thoughts or experiences of life when things got tough.

Share answers to these in small groups.

WORD-UP

These are the road signs of mindless Christianity. None of them are true but when things get tough in our faith, they can look as if they might be the obvious solutions.

Let's look at some of the things we can learn from the life of David.

BIBLE INVESTIGATION

Divide into three groups and look at the passages and questions as below:

Group 1

Read 2 Samuel 11: 1 to 12: 23 carefully!

Thinking about the Bible

1. What were the stages in David's fall into sin?
2. What were the stages in his repentance and restitution?
3. How did God use Nathan?

Thinking about yourself

1. When you find yourself slipping deeper into sin (no matter how small), are there similarities in the stages between what happens to you and what happened to David? Give examples if you can.
2. There was an element of punishment in the restitution. How do you feel about this attribute of God's nature – how does it influence your moral behaviour?

Group 2

Read 1 Samuel 24. (It may be worth scanning the preceding

chapters as well to see Saul's attempts on David's life and the extent of his jealousy.)

Thinking about the Bible

1. Discuss round your group: who would have taken the opportunity to kill Saul and who would have acted in the same way as David? Why?
2. What were the consequences for Saul of David's action?
3. What were the consequences for David of his action? (David became king and Saul died along with his sons in battle.)

Thinking about ourselves

1. David was obedient to God when he was tempted. What tempatations tend to draw us away from obedience?
2. David's men encouraged him to kill Saul, which is what Saul would have probably done if the situation had been reversed. What is the consequence for us if we listen to others rather than to God?
3. What do we learn from all this for when the going gets tough?

Group 3

Read 1 Samuel 17: 1–54. This is a well-known story, but try to read it carefully.

Thinking about the Bible

1. What was the Philistine strategy for undermining the people of God?
2. Why and how would David have been defeated if he had used Saul's weapons?

Thinking about ourselves

1. David defeated Goliath because he fought with his weapons, on his territory. What can we apply from this to our own spiritual battles?

2. What are the consequences for us of spiritual defeats and victories in our own personal life?

3. What do we learn about when the going gets tough in all this?

MODULE FIVE

The Holy Spirit
INTRODUCTION

The works and person of the Holy Spirit is an area where not only different denominations hold a variety of understandings and interpretations of Scripture but almost every church does as well! As Christians, we must be concerned that we are following biblical truth and that we are interpreting and acting upon what the Bible says as best we can. But still there seem to be diverse and strongly held opinions on the subject of the Holy Spirit.

The sessions in this teaching module look at some of the different aspects of the Holy Spirit. As youth leaders, we need to be balanced and honest in our teaching, especially if we know ourselves to belong to one particular view or understanding.

Like every other area we have looked at in our teaching modules, these sessions need to be translated into action:

- If we teach that God gives spiritual gifts to young people, do we allow them to use these gifts?
- If we teach the importance of prayer in spiritual warfare, do we hold regular youth prayer meetings, prayer walks, etc?

COMMON QUESTIONS

All this 'gifts stuff' seems a bit like magic?
Now, God and Jesus I can understand, but this Holy Spirit stuff?

Session 1
THE GIFTS OF THE HOLY SPIRIT

AIM

To learn more about the gifts of the Spirit, what they are and how to use them.

PREPARATION

Wrap up the present and forfeits for 'Pass the parcel', photocopy the Gift Sheet on p. 149, and borrow some toy and real garden implements.

WARM-UP

Pass the parcel

Play pass the parcel with a difference. You will find that with older teens you can get away with this in a way that you cannot with younger teens.

In the middle of the parcel you need to have quite a valuable gift (e.g. two cinema tickets, a CD or cassette voucher) and between the individual layers have some wicked 'forfeits'.

Before starting the game tell the group that the parcel is valuable and the forfeits wicked. A bit of a hard sell here can give a great feel to the game. Choose some background music to create a carnival feel.

Example forfeits

- Describe your most embarrassing moment
- Describe your least favourite toilet
- Propose to a member of the group
- Impersonate your minister preaching
- Kiss the first person on your left of the opposite sex
- Mime solo a romantic kiss with the person you love

MAIN SESSION

WORD-UP

Is pass the parcel sort of what Spiritual Gifts are about – quite valuable but so embarrassing discovering them that it makes you wonder if they are really worthwhile? This evening we will be trying to separate the 'cringe' from the 'charism' and the reality from the reactionary.

GIFT SHEET			
Gift	*Description*	*Useful for?*	*Dangers*
Words of knowledge	Information from God about a person or situation which is supernaturally given	Prayer ministry, guidance	Imagination, non-scriptural advice
Giving	Abundant giving to God beyond the 10%	God's work, where it lacks resources and prestige	Religious cons and charlatans exploiting people

Pass out the gift sheet, one to each person. Two of the gifts should already be filled in as shown above. The rest of the gifts can be found in:

1 Corinthians 12: 8–10
Romans 12: 3–8
1 Corinthians 13: 3
1 Corinthians 7: 7–8
1 Corinthians 12: 28
Ephesians 4: 8–14
1 Peter 4: 9

Allow everyone about twenty minutes (on their own or in pairs if they wish) to make as much progress as they can in filling out the sheet from the Bible references. Meanwhile, lay out on the floor a number of toy gardening implements and the real equivalents next to them.

SOUND BACK

Write up onto a flip chart or overhead projector a master Gift Sheet and fill it in briefly as each group reports back.

When everyone has reported back their findings, ask the whole group to put the gardening implements into an order of 'usefulness', the most useful being nearest one end of the room and the least useful being nearest the other. They are to include both the toy and genuine implements in their order. Obviously there will be some debate as to the usefulness of the toy gardening tools for someone with a large and overgrown garden!

ACTION

After the task has been completed ask the group to do the same thing to the master list of spiritual gifts for a society that has forgotten about God and is in a poor state of repair.

Discuss the reasons behind the priorities and choices they make.

OPEN FLOOR

Have an open discussion based on the following questions.

1. Is our use of spiritual gifts ever like playing with toys instead of using the real thing?
2. What gifts should we expect God to give us here in the youth group?
3. How can we effectively take God's gifts beyond the youth group and church?

Session 2
SPIRITUAL WARFARE

INTRODUCTION

Over recent years I have noticed an ever increasing amount of material available on spiritual warfare: books, tapes, seminars, etc. The quantity of literature is growing and new titles on this subject are appearing in the Christian bookshops: territorial spirits, prayer warfare, principalities and powers, etc. This literature is also now beginning to have its effect on our young people – most of them having read Peretti's *This Present Darkness*, *Piercing the Darkness* or similar titles. Suddenly they are asking new and far-reaching questions about topics that would not have arisen five or ten years ago. This greater awareness that they have is good, but it does have very real dangers. Yes, we do learn things from books but we must keep our young people balanced, realistic and wise in their warfare.

I remember one young person returning really angry from a Spring Harvest Optional Seminar on Spiritual Warfare. He had gone to the seminar because he had wanted to 'bash demons'. The seminar was excellent (I had gone myself) and had laid down the prerequisite for any action as holiness and a firm spiritual foundation and support system. It was just not what the young person had expected or wanted to hear. There is an almost fatalistic attitude now developing among young people because of this emphasis in discussions on spiritual warfare: it is all too easy either to say that the Devil is to blame for everything or to dismiss the whole thing altogether. Similarly, if we lay the blame for everything on demonic acitivity, then young people learn very quickly to cop out of any responsibility for their actions and their lives.

The Bible says that we wrestle against the world, the flesh and the Devil and more often than not our young people's failures are not 'because the Devil made me do it' but because of good, old-fashioned sin!

This rather long preamble to this session is to warn you, but also to encourage you. The battle is real but our prayers and the prayers of our young people really do make a difference. Young people with a balanced, wise and holy attitude to spiritual warfare make incredible warriors!

AIM

To investigate spiritual warfare – who is the fight against, what are the enemy's tactics and how do we fight back?

PREPARATION

You will need an ordinary pack of cards. Draw two copies of the Number Sheet (see below), large enough to put cards on. Photocopy a couple of copies of the Bible study cards.

MAIN SESSION: MYSTERY ATTACK

Divide the group into two equal teams. Each team has a sheet numbered 1–10 as below, large enough to put real cards on.

1	2	3	4	5	6	7	8	9	10

One team is given all the red cards from a pack of cards and the other team is given all the black ones.

The cards can be positioned on any of the numbers 1–10, either singly or in combinations. There are no rules as to where you must put the cards and how many you can put on any number. You can leave some numbers blank of cards if you wish. Each team has to decide how to distribute their cards on the Number Sheet.

The only rule at this stage is that each team should not see the other teams' cards.

When all the cards are positioned, a leader calls out 'Number one'. Each team counts up how many points they have resting on number one. (Number cards count as face value, Aces count 15, Kings count 13, Queens count 12, Jacks count 11.)

Each team will have allocated a number of cards to each square. The sum of the scores of those cards gives the value in terms of points on the square. The team with the most points on a given square in comparison with the opposition's points on the equivalent square, wins.

Every time a team conquers a number square they score a point as well as wiping out the opposition's cards.

After each round of all ten numbers, each team has to decide how to redistribute its remaining cards on the number sheet again. The game then starts again.

Play three or four rounds and add up the number of points each team has scored to find the winners.

If the game is totally one-sided, debrief and play again.

DEBRIEF

Debrief with the following questions:

Why did one team win?

What were the options discussed in the group?

Why did you choose the tactics you did?

What were the advantages and disadvantages of the tactics chosen?

WORD-UP

We sometimes imagine that spiritual warfare is rather like the game we have just played: the sides are equal, neither side knows what the other is doing, both have their own tactics and sometimes one wins and sometimes the other.

Is this really what we are talking about with spiritual warfare? What does the Bible say on the matter and what do we need for the fight?

BIBLE INVESTIGATION

Divide into small groups: pass one of the following cards out to each group. When they have finished a card give them another.

1. WHO IS THE ENEMY? 2 Corinthians 4: 4 Ephesians 2: 2 1 Peter 5: 8 John 12: 31 Ephesians 6: 12	2. WHAT ARE THE ENEMY'S TACTICS AND WEAPONRY? John 8: 44 Matthew 4: 1–11 Genesis 3 1 Thessalonians 3: 5
3. WHAT ARE OUR WEAPONS? Matthew 4: 1 2 Corinthians 10: 1–6 Ephesians 6: 1–20 1 John 3: 8	4. HOW DO WE PREPARE OURSELVES? Zechariah 4: 6 Mark 9: 25–29 1 John 2: 3

Let the small groups report back to the whole group one at a time.

WORD-UP

Explain that as Christians, spiritual warfare is a reality that we cannot ignore. The Devil is not God's equal, however; he is merely a fallen angel. On the cross, Jesus defeated the Devil and so in Jesus we can resist and then defeat the Devil's works.

Session 3
THE HOLY SPIRIT AND SIN

What sort of people can God use? Are the gifts of the Holy Spirit restricted to the 'Super Saints', while the rest of us, as second-class citizens, aren't in the same league? Or does it not matter what our spiritual or personal life is like: God is going to use us anyway? What impact does sin have on our openness to the Holy Spirit?

AIM

To look at how sin affects spiritual gifts.

PREPARATION

Photocopy the sheet on p. 156 and write the situations on p. 157 onto cards. Read up about the Holy Spirit.

WARM-UP

Hand out one 'How good are you?' sheet to everyone and ask them to fill it in (see example on p. 156).

When everyone has completed their sheets and translated their results onto the graphs, ask them to colour in the space on the bottom half.

WORD-UP

Ask if anyone had no space to colour in on their graph. (If anyone answers 'yes', ask the rest of the group if they think that is true!)

If the area we had to colour in could be seen as a measure of sin, then it is clear that none of us are sinless. This is our starting point for looking at openness to gifts.

HOW GOOD ARE YOU?

PUT AN 'X' ON THE LINE TO MARK YOUR POSITION BETWEEN THE TWO POINTS

A. *MONEY*

| All my money is available for God. | _____ | I do what I want with my money. |

B. *SEX*

| I never have impure thoughts. | _____ | I get off with whoever I want. |

C. *MY WAY*

| I am happy to follow God's will, whatever ... | _____ | I always want my own way |

D. *SERVANTHOOD*

| I look to others' needs first whenever I can | _____ | I do my thing ... they do theirs! |

E. *PARENTS*

| I honour my parents in all words and deeds | _____ | My parents have not earned any respect. |

F. *PRAYER*

| I am totally open to God in prayer | _____ | When I pray I tell God what I want |

WHEN YOU HAVE MARKED ALL YOUR POSITIONS, TRANSLATE THEM ONTO THE GRAPH BELOW AND COLOUR IN BELOW THE LINE

| A | B | C | D | E | F | EXAMPLE |

MAIN SESSION

Put the situation cards in the middle of the group.

Ask them to decide if God can use and empower each person.

---

1. A young worship leader who is sleeping with his girlfriend
2. Church warden embezzling his company
3. Young person beating up his brother
4. A young person who hates her mother
5. A member of a prayer group who envies her sister's clothes
6. One of an evangelistic team who lied to their parents
7. A national speaker who reads porn magazines
8. A cleric who reads his horoscope
9. A child abuser who has repented
10. You.

Allow a couple of minutes' discussion of a number of the cards before moving on to the Bible investigation exercise.

BIBLE INVESTIGATION

Divide the group into groups of three. Ask each group to consider the following:

What do each of these verses tell us about the Holy Spirit and sin?

1. Romans 3: 23
2. Genesis 3: 6–10
3. Colossians 3: 5–10
4. Romans 8: 22–27
5. Galatians 6: 16–22

After the groups have completed their investigation, look again at the situation cards. Do people feel differently about their decisions now?

WORD-UP

We are saved by grace, not by our own works or good deeds. It is the same when we are thinking about our openness to the gifts of the Holy Spirit. It is only if we are humble and penitent that God will endow us with his gifts (Luke 1: 48). Whether young or old, famous or not, it is a question of our availability. For most of us, it doesn't take long to slip from humble commitment to sinfulness. We can all too easily walk out of a meeting in which we have been used by God and be instantly overcome by pride or arrogance etc. But when we are open and expectant God can and does use us.

Session 4
THE HOLY SPIRIT: CHARACTER AND WORK

AIM

To investigate some of the characteristics of the Holy Spirit: what is the Holy Spirit like and what does the Holy Spirit do?

PREPARATION

Buy enough small chocolate bars, batteries, torch bulbs for each team of four to have one each. You will also need one blindfold and one plastic knitting needle per team.

WARM-UP

Divide into groups.

Each group should read the three verses from the Bible given below. These give us three descriptions of the Holy Spirit.

Matthew 3: 16

Acts 2: 2

Acts 2: 3

What characteristics of the Holy Spirit do we associate with each description?

Think of one description that is not true of the Holy Spirit and list the characteristics that would be associated with it.

Have the groups report back to share their findings and thoughts.

MAIN SESSION

Give each team of four (or five) a copy of the INSTRUCTIONS (below) and the equipment they will need (see PREPARATION on p. 158).

INSTRUCTIONS

Your challenge is to guide a member of your team, who should be blindfolded, in completing a task.

The task is to light the bulb provided using only the equipment which has already been given to you.

The bulb must remain lit after all team members have let go.

You have five minutes' planning time, during which you may not touch any equipment. After five minutes you must blindfold one of your team and the challenge will commence.

After the five minutes' planning time is up, inform the young people that the challenge is about to begin and check the blindfold.

Allow the team about five or ten minutes, depending on their age and ability, and then inspect the results. (The secret is to use the knitting needle to carve the chocolate and the foil wrapper to act as the conductor.)

After you have checked the results, allow them to eat the chocolate if they haven't done so already!

WORD-UP

The electrical circuit we created could be used as an illustration of the work of the Holy Spirit. In your groups come and choose a card.

On the card is an age-range or situation. Your task, as a team, is to plan and prepare a three-minute talk appropriate to that card. All the team must be involved in the planning of the talk, but not all have to speak. Your talk must be aimed at the group described on your card.

1. Church Club for five- to seven-year-olds
2. Open Club for eight- to ten-year-olds
3. Family Service
4. School Assembly
5. Service in an Old People's Home
6. Cub and Scout Service

When the talks are prepared, the groups are to give their talks to the whole group.

Close with prayer.

MODULE SIX

God, Jesus and other religions
INTRODUCTION

Of all those areas where we find the views of society differing from Christianity, by far the most difficult to teach about is the issue of Christianity and other faiths. When we say that there are not many paths up the one mountain, when we say that it *does* matter what we believe in, when we say that it *does* affect where you spend eternity if you accept or reject the claims of Jesus, we come up against immense opposition and incredulity. We are labelled 'fundamentalist', 'racist' or 'simplistic' and are told that surely we should realize that we now live in a more enlightened age.

Even if our views are not always popular, we need to teach the real issues and this is certainly one of the hottest potatoes around. Some of the issues that we will need to address in this module are:

1. Are all religions the same?
2. Does God speak through other religions?
3. Is Jesus really the only way?
4. Judgment: do people really go to heaven or hell?

COMMON QUESTIONS

During the course of this module you will no doubt be faced with a plethora of questions and points of dispute, which there isn't space to cover sufficiently here. Some thinking and preparation around the following may help you to be a little more prepared:

- If people hold their views sincerely, surely this is enough?
- Do we have the moral right to impose our views on someone else?
- Is it racist to say that people of other faiths are wrong?

Session 1
ARE ALL RELIGIONS THE SAME?

AIM

To demonstrate that the superficial similarities between religions do not hold up if we look at the beliefs and practices of the differing religions.

PREPARATION

Read up on World Religions. (*The Lion Guide to World Religions* and *Beliefs* by J Allen are both very useful books.)

WARM-UPS

Choose one (or both) of the following warm-up games.

Robots

Divide the group into two teams; one team are humanoid robots identical in every way to human beings except that there has been a mistake in their programming. The other team are human investigators who are trying to locate the robots. Line the teams up opposite and facing each other.

The robots are each given a characteristics card with their personal characteristic written on it. They must thereafter obey the instruction on the card.

The investigators ask questions of the robots. Investigators have to take it in turns to ask questions and they can question any robot.

At any stage in the proceedings, an investigator may make a guess at what a robot's characteristic is. Investigators are even permitted to make a guess when it isn't their turn to question.

When a robot's characteristic has been guessed, that robot is elminated.

Keep a score of how many questions each robot is asked before elimination and how many characteristics each investigator guesses.

The last robot remaining is the winner and the investigator who guesses the characteristic of the most robots also wins.

CHARACTERISTICS

Here are thirteen possible characteristics. Give each person on the robot team a card with one of these characteristics on it.

1. Just be yourself
2. Always lie in the answers you give.
3. Always mention the name of a sweet in the answer.
4. Always mention a part of the body in your answer.
5. Always answer with another question.
6. Answer as if you were one of the leaders.
7. Always ask the questioner to repeat or clarify the question.
8. Always include the word 'Right' in your answer.
9. Always sniff while answering.
10. Avoid the question and don't answer it.
11. Always cross your legs while answering.
12. Always include a number in your answer.
13. Always refer to one of your parents while answering.

WARM-UP 2

Sincerely snacking

Lay out on a table six bowls of 'potential' breakfast food; for example:

Porridge	Flour and water gruel
Cornflakes	Bird seed
Muesli	Dry cat food

Label the bowls 1–6.

Pass out a COMPARISON CARD to each person.

COMPARISON CARD (Give marks out of ten for each item)						
BOWL	1	2	3	4	5	6
Colour						
Nutritional value						
Fibre						
Smell						
Energy						
Taste						
TOTAL						

WORD-UP

There are a number of ways in which we can compare things. Either we can compare them on the grounds of what is similar to them (similarities) or on the grounds of what is different (differences). This is still true when we look at the many world religions.

MAIN SESSION

Pin up around the room six large sheets of paper (flip chart or similar) and label each with one of the world's religions. Beneath each place an enlarged copy of the questions outlined below.

1. How does a person become a member of this religion?
2. What does this world view tell us about God?

3. What purpose does this give to life?
4. What will happen when the follower of these beliefs dies?
5. How is this religion's belief expressed in:
   (a) action
   (b) morality
   (c) practice
6. In what countries is this faith held by over 5% of the population
7. How many people, worldwide, hold this faith?

Members go round the room and try to fill in the answers to the questions for each of the religions. (Yes, this is extremely difficult! How did you do?)

After everyone has had a chance to fill in any information that they are able to onto each of the big sheets, gather the sheets together at the front to look together at the information the group knows.

You could base the discussion around the following points.

1. Compare the areas of agreement and disagreement between faiths.
2. How does all this information help us to recognize that not all religions can be true?
3. How do the differences express themselves in the treatment of the poor, the old, the rich, etc.

CONCLUSION

In view of the differences that we have discovered, we now have to investigate how we can see Jesus as the only way to the Father.

Jesus: fact file

Jesus is unique:

1. He used 'I' when talking of God.
2. He forgave sins: something that only God could do.
3. He lived a sinless life but was tempted.
4. He died but was resurrected.

Session 2
DOES GOD SPEAK THROUGH OTHER RELIGIONS?

AIM

To continue to look at being a Christian in a multifaith world; providing our young people with tools and knowledge to challenge the modern pluralistic society view.

PREPARATION

Photocopy the group Bible studies and lay out ethnic foods.

WARM-UP

Have an ethnic food-tasting session. If there are any Asian or African Christians in your church or in a nearby church, invite them to come and cook (and share!), either at or just before your meeting.

Alternatively, you could visit an Asian sweet shop or other ethnic food shop and buy a variety of things to eat.

Talk about the following questions.

- What kind of foods did you like, and what flavours?
- What tastes didn't you like?
- Why or how do these tastes differ from the English equivalent (if they have an English counterpart)?
- What cultural, geographical or religious influences might affect the foods we have tasted?

MAIN SESSION

Divide the group into small Bible study groups and pass out the investigation cards.

Give the groups enough time to complete their section of the study and then let each of the groups report back briefly on their discoveries.

GROUP 1

Read Acts 17: 22–33,
Psalm 19: 1–4 and
Romans 1: 18–20.

1. How has God revealed
   himself?
2. What are people's
   responses to this
   revelation?
3. Have you had experi-
   ences of God revealing
   himself in this way?

GROUP 2

Read Romans 2: 12–15
and Matthew 7: 12.

1. How has God revealed
   himself?
2. What are people's
   responses to this
   revelation?
3. Have you had
   experiences of God
   revealing himself in this
   way?

GROUP 3

Read Ecclesiastes 3: 11
and Luke 18: 18–30.

1. How has God revealed
   himself?
2. What are people's
   responses to this
   revelation?
3. Have you had
   experiences of God
   revealing himself in this
   way?

GROUP 4

Read Acts 17: 22–33.

1. How has God revealed
   himself?
2. What are people's
   responses to Paul's
   preaching?
3. What can we apply to
   our own relationship
   with people of other
   faiths?

GROUP 5

Read Hebrews 1: 1–3 and
Hebrews 2: 1–4.

1. How has God revealed
   himself?
2. How have people
   responded to God's
   revelation?
3. What can we learn
   about relating to other
   faiths?

WORD-UP

The Bible tells us that God has revealed himself in a number of
ways:

- In creation: the universe; the very fact that we are here; the
  beauty of creation, mountains, sunsets . . . all these factors
  point to there being a Creator.
- In conscience: all of us have a sense of what is right and
  wrong, which is similar in every culture and ethnic
  grouping.
- A desire for eternity: we seem to be made with something
  within us that senses that there is an eternal dimension to
  our existence and that seeks after it, no matter what form
  that takes.
- A hunger for God: someone said that there is a need in
  everyone to worship. If that worship is not directed at the
  true object worthy of that worship, then we worship
  alternatives instead.

All these are ways in which, somehow, God has revealed himself generally. This revelation is evident for all to see but God
has revealed himself particularly and uniquely through:

- The prophets: God spoke to them and they spoke to others, revealing God's nature and his concerns.
- A son: Jesus was God incarnate; made flesh. God came to earth to seek after man and to reveal himself to man. Other religions have man seeking after God, in Christianity God is the initiator. Jesus is God's unique revelation. If we want to know about God then we need to get to know Jesus.

Session 3
IS JESUS THE ONLY WAY?

AIM

To demonstrate the biblical teaching that Jesus is the only way to the Father.

PREPARATION AND EQUIPMENT

Bibles, a one-inch-to-one-mile map (enough copies for one between every four or five people), cards with Bible verses on.

Photocopy the maps and instructions, prepare the Bible cards.

WARM-UP

Divide the group up into teams of four or five members and choose one of the warm-ups below.

Sincerely!

Each team nominates a couple to come to the front in turn and role-play one of the pair proposing to the other. The other teams give marks for believability and sincerity. In order for this to work, it needs to be fast and spontaneous.

DIY tasks

This warm-up is a team game based on accumulated individual times to complete various tasks. The first person from each team is given a task, e.g. changing a plug. They can all do the task at the same time but each person has to

complete the task against the clock. After they have finished
and the times have been recorded, the second member of each
team comes out and is given a different task (see table below):

	Team 1	Team 2	Team 3	Team 4
Person 1	Change plug	Insert screw	Change tap washer	Chisel brick in half
Person 2	Chisel brick in half	Change plug	Insert screw	Change tap washer
Person 3	Change tap washer	Chisel brick in half	Change plug	Insert screw
Person 4	Insert screw	Change tap washer	Chisel brick in half	Change plug

Total all the time points at the end to see who the winner is.
(The winner is the team with the smallest total time score at the
end of the game.) If tasks fail to be completed, agree on a
standard time to award . . . ten minutes . . . an hour!

Journeys

Give each team an identical copy of a portion of a one-inch-to-
one-mile Ordnance Survey Map, complete with instructions
and grid references.

The aim of the exercise is to plan the route of a walk from 'X'
to 'Y' as marked on the map. Each team should be given the
same route to plan and the exercise should be planned as if
they were really to walk the route, taking into consideration
stops and camping facilities, as the whole distance would be
too far to be walked in one day. Tailor the route and
considerations according to the abilities and knowledge of
your group and give them help where necessary.

Ask teams to report back on the routes they have chosen and
why.

MAIN SESSION

Is Jesus to be seen as a route from 'X' to 'Y' and just one route among many possible routes? Christianity has always taught that Jesus is the only way.

Prepare a set of six cards with Bible verses for each team. All the teams should have the same six Bible verses. You could use a different colour card for each team to avoid confusion.

One person from each team comes and collects the first Bible verse. They have to take it back to their team, look it up and decide, from the verse, how we get to heaven. They write down the answer and then come up for the second verse, and so on until all teams have finished. Spend a short time sharing some of the discoveries.

The verses are:

John 14: 6	Ephesians 2: 8–9	1 Timothy 1: 15
Acts 2: 21	Romans 10: 13	1 Peter 3: 21

CONCLUSION

Draw the session together using the following to link in the Bible discoveries and any of the warm-ups used at the beginning.

1. Sincerity is not the issue. Salvation is only found through Jesus. Many of the other religions do not even have salvation as something that is offered in any real sense.

2. DIY: Doing good things, striving to be a good person and being 'religious' is not the issue either. We cannot earn a place in heaven as some religions teach. Eternity in heaven is a free gift.

3. Salvation is found only through Jesus, and because of this there really cannot be much point following any other path. After all, we wouldn't even be following another route because of altruistic reasoning motives such as wanting to serve others, because some other religions do not have provision for this.

Session 4
HEAVEN OR HELL?

AIM

To investigate the concepts of heaven and hell.

PREPARATION AND EQUIPMENT

Large sheets of paper, paint and art and craft supplies.

WARM-UP: PICTURE IT!

Pass out to everyone large sheets of paper, paints, brushes and any craft supplies you have chosen. Ask everyone to produce a picture, representation or image of heaven and hell.

After the pictures have been completed give everyone the chance to say something about theirs and to show it to the rest of the group.

WORD-UP

Where do all these images that we hold in our heads about heaven and hell come from? (Allow time for a brainstorm of ideas here onto a large sheet of paper or onto an overhead projector screen.) Are they from record album covers, Milton's *Paradise Lost*, Renaissance art, horror videos, or where? Are they based on biblical imagery?

MAIN SESSION

1. In pairs, read Luke 16: 19–31, and think about these two questions:
   What does this passage tell us about what hell is like?
   What was the rich man able to do in hell and what was he unable to do?

2. Read Revelation 21: 1–27, and think about these two questions:
   What does this passage tell us about what heaven is like?
   Who does this passage say will be in heaven?

Allow people time to report back their findings to the whole group, to share any surprises they had and to ask any questions that have sprung up so far.

WORD-UP

One of the hardest questions we may ever have to ask ourselves is who will go where when we die, and what the criteria are when we try to decide.

It is important to remember the following:

1. God decides

God is always totally just and fair and he can be relied on because of this.

2. God values free will

God will never override our free will. Those who choose to reject Jesus are also choosing to be separated from him after Judgment because they have the free will and responsibility to decide. God knows the motivations behind our actions and decisions. Ultimately, he will judge us on the contents of our hearts.

3. Those who have never heard

'What about those who don't know about God and Jesus?' is a question that echoes in everyone's mind at the mention of this topic.

Some may have prayed as the tax man in the parable, 'God have mercy on me, a sinner' and then have, as Jesus said, 'gone home justified'. Whatever we decide, it is God who decides about heaven and hell and we shall never know how. He is fair. Whatever we think that we feel about the criteria, should never override the imperative to take the news of the Gospel to everyone.

FIVE

Radical Action

*Do not merely listen to the word and so
deceive yourself. Do what it says.*
James 1:22 [NIV]

To reach maturity in Christ, we have to put our Christianity into practice. It is only when they apply the 'theory' to real-life circumstances that young people begin to discover exactly what it is that they really believe, as against what they simply assent to mentally.

It is easy for a young person to say that he or she believes that God values everyone, but it is not quite so easy for them to mop up vomit at a handicapped children's crèche. It is easy for them to say that sex before marriage is wrong when they have not got a girlfriend or boyfriend, but it is a different prospect when the guy or girl whom they love is putting on the pressure. All too often, the lesson that is taught on a Sunday evening in the safe and familiar atmosphere of a youth group begins to fall apart when the young person experiences temptation or opposition in the world beyond church.

As youth leaders, we need to help bridge the gap by providing opportunities for our young people to put their faith into action: to develop the disciplines of prayer and Bible study on the front line, to show them that the Gospel is not about just saying the right words but about doing Jesus' will – which is a whole lot harder!

This chapter pulls together some of the ways in which we can help this process happen. Some ideas have been borrowed from other youth groups or from fellow leaders; others are

National Resources that are too good not to encourage you to get involved with; and others come from the work that I have been involved in.

One last thought . . . Radical Action can be good for you as a youth leader! Although the preparation process may exhaust you emotionally, physically and mentally, it will also be something that builds you up. Some of the best moments in my youth ministry so far have been when we have taught on something at youth group and the young people have gone on to put it into practice. I have been able to sit and watch and say, 'Father God, thank you for what they are doing – and bless them.' It may be the dance group in action, it may be the youngsters out on the streets, campaigning, unicycling or busking for God, it may be watching them lead worship at church or deciding to give up a year for God or it may be their deciding not to make the same mistake again. Whatever the event or scale, it's great!

MONEY RAISERS

Fund-raising is the most common way in which most youth groups get involved in Radical Action. The funds may be raised for a variety of causes; there are as many worthy causes as there are methods of raising the money itself. It could be in aid of local or national charities, mission organizations or perhaps to support a fellow young person giving time for God. Raising funds is often more effective where there is an established connection between the recipient of the money and those involved in the action.

For any fund-raising event to be successful it needs a number of ingredients: participation, preparation and publicity.

Participation The exercise will be useless if all the work is left either to a tiny group of people or to you as youth leader! The group will need to be able to 'own' their project and this will only come about with as many members as possible taking part. Their involvement and enthusiasm will rub off on others and not only result in the event being more successful but also in the whole event being much more enjoyable.

Preparation Who is going to do what? Venues may need to be booked as much as six to twelve months in advance for big events. Permission letters may need to be written and sent to parents and, above all, time and effort will need to be spent to enthuse the young people about their project.

This all means planning meetings and time given in advance, which can all too easily disrupt the youth programme if not catered for carefully.

Publicity Good publicity can be the making or breaking of many events. Publicity does not just mean effective posters or articles in the church magazine; it also means utilization of the facilities and readership of the local press. Local papers are often keen for youth stories and therefore a good relationship with local reporters may be invaluable and needs to be cultivated. Don't be afraid or put off by them, they really don't bite and you are often doing them a favour too! Local radio is another great but often under-utilized medium for publicity. Use 'What's on' or 'Diary' announcements and, if you are able to arrange it, interviews and chat sessions. Often young people can be far more effective than the youth leaders in getting access to the media, so let them have a go and you may be pleasantly surprised!

Some dangers of fund-raising events

There are some dangers which need to be kept in mind.

1. Schools today utilize a wide range of fund-raising events, both for themselves and for other worthwhile causes, through discos, non-uniform days, sponsored events and the like.

2. If we have too many fund-raising events, we may inadvertently give the impression that money is the most

important thing: we live in a culture that worships at the altar of Mammon, and as Kingdom people of God we must provide an alternative.

3. One question to keep in mind is, 'Who is the money coming from?' Are our fund-raising attempts always drawing on the same pool of people either for money or their time and energy? The danger of too many sponsored or sale events is that it becomes the young people's parents or a small section of the congregation that is constantly paying out.

Some advantages of fund-raising events

But the advantages include:

1. Young people have a common experience of fund-raising through Comic Relief, Telethon and school experiences; they know what it is all about and have resources and memories which they are able to draw on.

2. The low level of spiritual commitment required enables fund-raising to be an activity where non-Christians can be involved and can enjoy without being pressured etc.

3. Fund-raising ideas are adaptable to any size of youth group. You can have a sponsored fast with two members or two hundred!

4. Fund-raising gets people working together and focused on the task. Sometimes they provide the opportunity to talk to people about the meaning behind what is being done.

5. Fund-raising is a good introduction to Radical Action, but one that should also provide a base for some more *adventurous* activities.

SALES AND AUCTIONS

Almost anything can be sold. When I was a child, we set up a flower stall outside our house selling the contents of the garden to passing motorists. This did not really go down a bundle with my Mum and Dad but it did raise some money! I suppose the moral of the story is: before you begin, make sure you have the right to sell what you are selling!

YOUTH GROUP COOKBOOK

Why not produce your own cookbook for sale to the congregation, parents or at the Christmas Fayre, etc. Each member of the group produces a couple of proven recipes; they could be for their favourite biscuits or cake, cheap student food, romantic favourites or Granny's 'secret' recipe. These are collated and typed (and perhaps illustrated?) by the youth group to produce a master copy of the book which may be photocopied or printed depending on the number of copies you require and on your budget. Make the book any size you wish (A5 size is quite convenient) and add a card cover, which can be stapled or bound to produce a smart end product.

Selling and marketing this book will not only raise some money but will encourage the group to work together on a project and raise their profile amongst the congregation.

CAKE BAKE

This ever-popular fund-raiser comes in a variety of flavours: ranging from the basic 'cook your cake at home and bring for sale at church the next day', to 'everyone cooks their cakes at the church hall the night before'. Combine this with a sleep-over and the challenge is to stay awake through the church service the next morning to sell them! (Perhaps you could add a competitive edge to the exercise: males versus females and see who can raise the most.) Usually all cakes are sold at great speed, but if they don't all sell, you can always have the added bun fight at the youth fellowship meeting in the evening!

VALENTINE SERENADE

If you have talented musicians or singers in your group why

not advertise this unique service in the January church magazine or on the notice boards?

For a fixed fee (£5 or £10) you will provide the perfect accompaniment to a romantic meal at home or in a restaurant. Your barbershop singers (or violinists or whatever) will come and provide a unique serenade for about three to five minutes for you and that someone special in your life – boyfriend, girlfriend, neighbour, Mum or Dad, dog.

This fund-raiser will need careful administration and a well-planned booking procedure to ensure adequate travel time is left between engagements. Permission may need to be acquired to perform in restaurants or at street corners or under bedroom windows, etc. From a large group you may be able to provide a variety of serenade styles to suit most people, but do make sure that the groups are good to ensure a quality service worth paying for!

SLAVE SALE

Many parents often voice the opinion that their young people treat the family home like a hotel and the car like a taxi service. This is the ideal opportunity for them to get their own back and raise money at the same time. Good publicity in advance should ensure that both parents and congregation will be bidding up the prices high at the Annual Youth Group Sale.

You will need an auctioneer, a master of ceremonies and a very willing youth group. The idea is that members of the group are auctioned off as slaves for a given period of time. An auctioneer with a good patter and the gift of the gab can make this exceptionally funny without being hurtful, by extolling the strengths and good characters of the slaves to get the best prices. Whoever bids the highest price may have their slave peeling potatoes, cleaning windows, washing cars, raking leaves or gardening. In addition to raising money, this fund-raiser often allows relationships to develop between adults and young people, parents and congregation members.

TALENT SALE

This is a similar idea to the Slave Auction: the young people compile a list of skills and the amount of time that each member is willing to donate, e.g. two hours fixing washing machines, five hours babysitting, three hours of sumo wrestling training, etc. Then these skills and talents are auctioned off as above.

JUNK SALE

Perhaps you could hold a once-a-year Junk Sale in which the young people bring along their unwanted but saleable possessions: e.g. *Take That* posters, video games, discarded clothes, single ear-rings. Have a price for each type of item, publicize the event and let the young people run it.

SPONSORED EVENTS

I have to confess to not being a great fan of sponsored events. This may be because I was seriously conned by my first youth group into running the Leicester Marathon – sponsored of course! I spent six gruelling months training to get into condition and on the day of the race finished spectacularly to be interviewed by the local radio as I crossed the finishing line – last! As I surveyed my bruised and blistered feet, the hours of training and the amount of sponsorship, I think I would much rather have written a cheque!

As well as all the usual sponsored events, there are endless possibilities, but try to be inventive. You can fast, have litter picks, Bible read-a-thons, quiz nights, hair and beard cuts, bike rides, 'bop 'til you drop' evenings, walks and so on.

STATIONARY BIKE RIDE

To support a project in a particular area (e.g. digging a well in an Ethiopian village) why not arrange a sponsored cycle ride there? Work out the route to take, which countries to cross and how many miles it will be. (Remembering that the miles up mountains take longer!)

Set up an exercise bike in the hall and put up plenty of information about the project concerned and, of course, the vital map to chart progress as it happens. Arrange riders in relay to get you to your destination.

Sponsorship could be taken per mile, or for the length of time it takes to get to the destination. Sponsorship could even be for a percentage of the journey.

Variation 1

Make a comprehensive list of equipment that would be needed if the journey was to be physically undertaken and also how much the items would cost. The journey itself cannot be undertaken until money has been pledged or given to purchase the items on the list. This could become a larger project with the youth group raising smaller amounts of money for each item over a long period of time.

Variation 2

In line with both of the above, make a list of aid or supplies that are needed by the project or aid agency you are planning to support (e.g. thirty blankets or boxes of food, toiletries), and have people either pledge to pay for goods on the list or donate items as required. As a result, in addition to the funds raised by the journey, you will have supplies to send to the agency you are supporting. The accumulation of supplies has a lovely practical and solid feel to it, and some people feel more able to contribute bars of soap than sums of money in sponsorship.

SPECIAL EVENTS

You might consider putting on a really special, one-off event.

JAZZ BAND BALL

This is an upmarket fund-raiser. We raised over £1,000 towards a non-alcoholic bar with this. We hired a town hall and decked it out with good quality decorations, flowers and greenery, and then hired a jazz band to provide the music. Wherever we could, we begged and borrowed items. Invitations and free tickets were sent to the local Mayoress, our MP and the press, while the remaining tickets were sold to parents, church members' friends and, in fact, anyone who could be persuaded to buy one. The tickets were not cheap (around £10) but then it was a high-class event and people expected to pay.

On the evening itself, all the members dressed in dinner suits and ballgowns and served behind the bar (non-alcoholic, of course), manned a display about the project being supported and welcomed people as they arrived. The press gave the event a favourable write-up. The net result was money for the project concerned, a positive image within the community and a great time had by all ages and a cross-section of the community together.

FASHION SHOW

There are several different ways of doing this: money can be raised from the sale of tickets, from gifts from participating companies and also from refreshments and other sales at the event.

The hard work for your young people is persuading local companies to participate. (Of course, if some of your group have Saturday jobs at local clothes shops, this can be a big plus.) A venue has to be chosen, booked and then suitably decorated, and tickets have to be designed, printed and sold. Publicity is very important for this event, so much thought and creativity needs to be put in here. Find someone to be the compère for the evening, and if you have a local personality or celebrity who could open the event, that would be great.

A further question to ask is, 'Who should model the clothes?' Obviously this will be dependent upon the kind of group you have. On principle, my view is that anyone who would like to should get the chance. Unlike the fashion industry, we don't want to discriminate on grounds of height, weight, size, looks, etc. Do be careful as these can be sensitive issues. If you cannot find enough volunteers from within the youth group, open it up to friends and people from school, etc.

On the actual evening you will need people to be on the door to take tickets, show guests to their seats and serve refreshments. The whole event can be quite hard to organize, but it can raise money and awareness for projects that really matter while everyone has a lot of fun.

ANTIQUE AUCTION

This can be a great all-age church activity in support of a Third World project or Mission scheme. The youth group can provide the organization and motivation as well as the muscle.

The congregation is invited to give unwanted items of furniture, clocks, ornaments, tables, pictures and the like. These are collected before the auction (perhaps the day or evening before) to give time for someone to come in and give professional valuations of all articles. Any item of particular value (you never know what might turn up!) should go to a professional auction for sale.

Lay out all the items after they have been allocated lot numbers and open the doors several hours before the sale to allow prospective bidders to survey the goods.

Good publicity will ensure a good crowd. The job of auctioneer is a skilled one and if you don't have someone who is experienced at the task it may well be worth trying to find someone who knows a bit about what they are doing to ensure that the event runs smoothly.

Obviously your youth group will not be able to hold an event like this on a regular basis, but with careful planning and publicity and a good hoard of items, the event can be exciting and profitable.

NATIONAL PROJECTS

There is a great value sometimes in tapping into events, projects and initiatives that are taking place nationally. It helps young people to feel part of something larger, broadens their horizons, and gives them the opportunity to have different experiences and to be exposed to different influences. Help your young people to evaluate the schemes that are available and to develop their own ideas and local initiatives. Sometimes they will latch onto concepts and action far more readily when they are put forward by a national organization and in a fun way, and at other times they will look to you for reassurance that what they are experiencing is OK. Either way, national organizations provide a wealth of experience and resources which you can use in many ways.

In this section there are a few examples of projects that can help you and your young people to put faith into action. This is by no means a definitive list, and there are a great many other organizations and initiatives doing equally good things. The ones described here, however, have been used by the youth groups I have had contact with, and so I have experienced their value first hand.

THIRD TRACK

One national organization that produces material for use in youth groups is Tear Fund. As well as the usual videos, posters and Tearcraft goods, they also produce *Third Track:* a resource especially for youth groups.

I have to admit to being a little biased: *Third Track* is excellent, a first-class and brilliant resource that every Christian youth leader with a commitment to Third World issues should seriously think about receiving. It is not just full of challenging and informative material, action ideas and suggestions, poems, facts, session outlines and helpful ways in which to present your material, but after the first £3 it is free! It is published three times a year, and each issue concentrates on different topics. Your £3 also gets you a starter pack of several past issues. It is an ideal way of mobilizing your young people.

When you have received your starter pack, ask your young people if any of them are interested in leading a evening's session on a particular topic. Get a small group together and give them the *Third Track* material. (They are allowed to photocopy it if they wish to in order to have a copy each but it is more environmentally friendly to pull it apart and give everyone a page.) The young people use the material (and anything else relevant that they can find) to plan, prepare and run the youth group session. If they enjoy the experience and the group does too, perhaps have members run *Third Track* evenings twice a term. Your young people will become enlightened, informed and active. The material provided is varied enough to keep their interest and challenging enough to spark off ideas for further sessions and projects which they can initiate and carry out themselves.

You can get hold of *Third Track* from:

Resources
Tear Fund
100 Church Road
Teddington
Middlesex TW11 8GE

BREAD FOR LIFE (TEAR FUND)

This is another excellent project pioneered by Tear Fund. It is concerned with making a real difference to the lives of hungry people by providing healthy food supplies, farming and nutrition advice to thousands of people. As the name implies, *Bread for life* is a food programme. It can be supported with a small financial commitment by your group – £7.50 a month. For this amount you receive an Action Pack and a feedback newsletter three times a year.

Your group can raise the money in a number of ways: by

using standard (or more inventive!) fund-raisers, by using the 'Miss a Meal' (see Third World action) option or from tithing subs to youth group. Further details can be obtained by contacting Tear Fund at the address above.

IT'S LIFE JIM

This is a fabulous opportunity for your youth group to plan, run and then participate in an event. The scheme is resourced by the Shaftesbury Society, who describe it in this way:

It's Life Jim consists of holding an alternative party along the lines of a lock-in: 8.00 pm-8.00 am, with music, videos, games, competitions, a 'Bop till you Drop' fund-raiser, thoughts and discussions about disABILITY (one of the Shaftesbury Society's main areas of work), live music from local Christian bands, food, etc. An event to which your youth group can bring their non-churchgoing friends and all have a great time.

The whole event is geared to take place on Hallowe'en each year. It is really up to you and your group how much of the support material of videos, cassettes, publicity, etc, you use. If you have the time, why not go beyond a one-night event and make a whole weekend of it?

As I see it the strengths of this type of event are:

1. It hits hard the issues of disability, which we often steer clear of in youth groups.

2. It can be run *by* your young people *for* other people. This gives them the experience of preparing and then running the event and they still get to participate. This makes for far more effective evangelism.

3. It is a great way to involve non-churchgoing young people, both in the preparation (if they have the skills and talents required, e.g. lighting, electricals, DJs, etc) and in taking part.

For further details contact:

Peter Hutchinson
The Shaftesbury Society
18–20 Kingston Road
London
SW19 1JZ
Telephone: 081–542 5550

CHRISTMAS CRACKER

It was about six weeks before Christmas 1989 when we took over the disused wine bar on the corner of the derelict shopping arcade. In two weeks the young people had painted it, decorated it, laid a floor, cleaned, scrubbed and prepared it, fitted a kitchen, begged, borrowed and bought food, invited an unknown pop star to open the joint and informed the press. We were part of the *Christmas Cracker Project* with our own Eat Less, Pay More restaurant.

Christmas Cracker was a great project for our young people to be involved in. It used a huge variety of gifts and skills in setting up, planning and finally running the restaurant.

'Eat Less, Pay More' Restaurants, 'Tune in pay out' radio, 'Crackerteria' and 'Really Useful Present Stores' have all been part of *Christmas Cracker* and have succeeded in raising millions of pounds for projects overseas. Steve Chalke of Oasis Trust writes:

Church youth groups throughout Great Britain have wholeheartedly invested their time and energy on behalf of their needy brothers and sisters around the world. Now, whether it's in the slums of Bombay or on the streets of Brazil or in the war-torn areas of Africa and Croatia, *Cracker* is making a difference by helping Christians there to launch or continue vital relief and development projects.

But besides raising money, helping the Third World Church in its work, supporting projects which have an emphasis on the whole person and motivating and inspiring a new generation to world concern and mission, *Cracker* is also about challenging attitudes and changing lifestyles.

This has to be what Radical Action really is about. If you haven't cracked a *Cracker*, contact Oasis for further information:

Christmas Cracker
Oasis (West Midlands)
Cornerstone House
5 Ethel Street
Birmingham
B2 4BG

THIRD WORLD ACTION

DISPLAY IT

Create a display on a development issue and find a number of building societies or shops that would be willing to host it for a week as part of an awareness-raising programme. You should keep the following points in mind:

1. Ensure that the display is of very good quality.
2. Opt not only for posters but also for tangible items: coffee beans, newspapers, Third World crafts – whatever is relevant to the theme of the display.
3. Have a contact number or address for those who see the display and who would like more information.
4. If you decide to advertise your display or the entire programme in the local press, remember to mention the building society or shop.
5. Don't forget to say 'thank you' to your display hosts!

FAIR TRADING

Young people are consumers, and how they spend their money does have an impact. Their commitment to fair trade can help the poor and oppressed overseas.

There are a growing number of goods that can be purchased from organizations like Tearfund, Traidcraft and Oxfam; some supermarkets stock goods that are marked to indicate their commitment to fair trade. These include brands of coffee, tea, pulses, nuts, etc. These are products where a fair price is paid to producers in the Third World.

Obviously in cases where young people are living at home with parents, purchase of some of these items will involve negotiation with parents. Involvement in this kind of project by members will mean that they will have to be sure of what exactly they are doing and the reasons that they are doing it. Provide lots of support and information on the issues concerned, and your young people may surprise you with their commitment to fair trade.

MISS A MEAL

This combines Third World action with opportunities for fund-raising and starting conversations with people about the issues concerned and supported. The concept is simple. All that is involved is a decision to miss lunch or dinner on just one day a week. The money saved is given to a good cause of the participants' choice.

This simple idea has numerous strengths, one being giving young people an opportunity to develop personal discipline. We live in an 'I've got to have it and have it now' society, and challenges that allow our young people to develop will-power and self-control are invaluable.

Missing just one meal is in a small way an attempt to identify in a practical way with the millions of people who go without food each day. It does not do any harm to the young people if done carefully. (Obviously, those with certain medical conditions where missing a meal may be harmful should not participate. For young group members, it would probably be helpful to gain parental permission.)

BABY MILK ACTION

One and a half million babies die every year because they are not breast-fed. (UNICEF.)

Many people feel strongly about the marketing policies used

by baby milk manufacturers in the Third World, where new mothers are given free powdered milk while they are in hospital so that their babies do not learn to breast-feed. When they leave hospital, the mothers find themselves having to buy powdered milk at prices they can ill-afford. As a result, babies are fed less, they become malnourished and prone to even fatal diseases.

If your group feels strongly about this, you can get an information pack from Baby Milk Action:

Baby Milk Action
23 St Andrew's Street
Cambridge
CB2 3AX
Telephone: (0223) 464420

WASH FOR DOSH

The youth group were busy brainstorming ideas for their Wash for Dosh evening. How about washing the Bull on the Bull Ring or the Statues in Centenary Square? Anyone got a pet elephant that we could wash?' The reality was a school minibus, some children, a bird bath and some cars, windows and kitchen floors.

Christian Aid's 'Wash for Dosh' is their *Wipe Out Poverty* project. This is another opportunity for your youth group to get themselves into action and raise money for projects in the Third World. Christian Aid's material on the 'Wash for Dosh' project says:

'It's simple – register yourself or your group and we'll send you a free fund-raising kit with your own *Wipe Out Poverty* cloths. Use the cloths to clean, wash and wipe for money by getting sponsored or paid per job.

Anyone can join in. *Wipe Out Poverty* can be done just by individual friends, families or classmates. It's even better as part of a group in churches, schools, workplaces, colleges and clubs.

Either: get sponsored for the number of things that you clean, how long the job takes or to beat a challenge.

Or: get paid a good price per job.
Or WHY NOT TRY BOTH??'

For more details contact:

Wipe Out Poverty
Christian Aid
PO Box 100
London
SE1 7RT

Or simply 'phone Kevin or Neil on the Wipe Out Poverty Hotline on 071–620 4444 (Monday to Friday) (after hours: 071–928 0710)

EVANGELISTIC ACTION

Today's culture in the world of young people is both pluralistic and privatized (i.e. what you believe is up to you and your own personal thing). With this world view, it follows that imposing your beliefs, value system, etc upon someone else has become something of an anathema. Evangelism is usually not only something that our young people (and leaders!) often feel easier talking about than doing, but also something that is quite alien. Often, as youth leaders, we share our group's apprehension about evangelism, and if you are considering skipping this section because it is unfamiliar and uncomfortable, hang in there for a bit and get radical!

Over the years we have had the privilege of seeing many young people become Christians from a variety of situations and backgrounds. They have made their commitments at much the same events as young people always have done: youth services, house parties, residentials, school missions, evangelistic rallies, national events, etc. However, the main reason (the backbone, if you like) seems to have changed. The critical factor has not been the quality of the evangelist who was preaching, the nature or content of his talk or even how good the band was. The overriding reason why young people today seem to become Christians is their discovery of a God whom they see as real in the lives of the other Christian young people they come into contact with. As one young person put it, 'I looked at the way you all cared for one another. Whatever it was that you had, I wanted it.'

When the young people come to youth services or go to Spring Harvest or similar events, the event itself is merely the culmination of a process: a process of identifying that they were missing something, what that something was and that the something was a product of Jesus.

What this all means for us as youth leaders is that evangelism becomes less a question of what we can do to get them in, but more a case of what can we do to get out there. If it is the quality of relationships and the real presence of God that attracts people, then those things are what we should be involved with and pouring our energy into. This section gives ideas to help us begin to think about how to do this in our local communities.

JUST-LOOKING GROUPS

Members invite friends round or meet up at school to run a just-looking group. (We have found that this has worked well with sixth form and with older young people.) The idea is that non-Christian young people meet in groups (usually led by Christian young people) for a short and agreed length of time with the intent of finding out more about Christianity in a no-pressure situation.

The groups meet to look at the life, teaching, death and resurrection of Jesus, and also to discuss and find out more about what a Christian actually is. They do this through Bible study and discussion (or chat) times.

At the end of this short course, the young people are encouraged to find out more (only if they are interested) by coming along on a Sunday evening. They are, however, free to leave their exploration there and should feel no pressure to do otherwise.

This course is also ideal for those members (or fringe

members) of your youth group who are not quite sure about what they believe or who would like a refresher course.

T-SHIRTS

Having T-shirts with a logo for your group on them can be a useful and interesting evangelistic tool as well as a fun activity for the group itself.

A few years ago, our Youth Worship Band produced distinctive black sweatshirts with the name of the band on the front and the wearer's instrument or role on the back (e.g. sound crew, roadie, trumpet, vocals). Not only were young people keen to be involved in the band and associated ministries of prayer team, dance and drama, but the shirts themselves provided opportunities for them to have to explain what they were doing and why. Questions ranged from 'What does "Mushite Clan" mean?' (you will have to find it for yourself!) to 'How come there are so many young people involved in something churchy when the church is meant to be full of old people?'

T-shirts can also be used as a discussion starter at joint youth events (spiritual or secular). Some of our young people took part in an all-night challenge organized by Youth Clubs UK and the local association of youth clubs. The T-shirts our team wore had *3:16* on the front and *Know what I mean, John* on the reverse. As our team explained at the end, 'We did not win because we were too busy talking to people about what the T-shirts mean!'

T-shirts can provide an identity for your group, confidence for quieter members to be identified with a larger, more confident contingent wearing them, and also an evangelistic tool that is not embarrassing to young people.

SCHOOL ACTION

The hardest place to be a Christian today for young people is in school. The Christian Union at my local secondary school contains members from fifteen different churches; they are often the only one from that church at the school. Until the Christian Union began, most of them did not realize that the others were Christians at their school.

This is all too often the situation. Without a credible Christian Union, young people feel isolated and defensive. Radical Action at school needs to take into account the vulnerable and exposed position of many of our young people at school. Alongside this, we have to realize that school is the place where young people can be most effective in outreach to their peers, but they need our support and our prayers as they are on the front line, and this is a dangerous place to be.

PRAYING TOGETHER

The starting place for all school ministry has to be one of prayer. Young people need to be encouraged to pray for their school together, both on and off the premises. We as youth leaders and church members need to pray for our young people and help them in all ways that we can.

In school, your young people will need a place to pray, meet and share. A classroom is good but, if that proves to be impossible, any space will do. They will soon learn that there is more to prayer than 'hands together, eyes closed'.

How can you as a youth leader help? Listen, encourage (all the time), pray for them and ensure that your church prays for them.

There are a number of youth group projects that can spill over into school. These include:

- World Vision Fast
- Fair Trading
- Miss-A-Meal
- It's Life Jim
- Christmas Cracker
- Environmental Action
- Community Action

But what can Christians do specifically in schools?

ASSEMBLIES

Most teachers do not enjoy doing assemblies and most of the young people abhor attending them, so a group of pupils taking an assembly is always a popular variation. The young people will know what might work and what definitely will not, but they will probably need help: they may *say* that everyone hates being preached at but could nevertheless produce an assembly that does just that! If a group of young people are to do regular assembly slots, you may be required to provide resources, although my experience is that the young people are often more resourceful and innovative themselves.

So, as a youth leader, how do you sell this one to the youth group? Imagine: 'OK, guys, I want three of you to take the school assembly next Wednesday; don't worry, I'll be praying for you!'

Let's be real! It won't happen that way around. Our young people need to see the opportunity or have the desire to reach their friends before we make suggestions as to how this should be done. The desire will come only as the Holy Spirit changes and transforms the hearts of the young people. Our teaching and youth work encourages them to be open to God and grow in that commitment.

The time may come when we make the suggestion ourselves to an individual or to a house group. One of the arts of being a youth leader is that of making suggestions that are already lying dormant inside the members. Their response initially may not be a positive one but long after they have forgotten that you first suggested it to them, they suggest it to you as a great idea that they have had, and can you help them with it! The idea was suggested by you but now has been owned and developed by them.

FOOTWASHING

Some of our Christian youth decided to put the lessons of John

13 into action in a very literal fashion at school one lunchtime by washing the feet of their fellow students. This caused quite a stir and a number of conversations about why they were doing it, which led to discussions about what Christianity is about.

Footwashing does not have to be such a literal act; any act of service towards other students can be a valuable demonstration of Christ's servanthood and sacrificial love for us, however lowly and unpopular. When I went to work at a community school, the vice-principal commented that there was a group of Christian students who were highly involved in the community projects and a real asset – he was right!

ALTERNATIVE TUCK SHOP

Many schools run tuck shops. If there are sufficient group members at a school, they could open an alternative tuck shop for a week. This could be to raise money for a project or to raise awareness about an issue.

Alternative tuck shops can serve home-produced food or fairly traded food or healthy alternatives to chocolate and chips, etc. Youth group members can design posters and prepare the food beforehand even if they are not at the same school. Your young people will need to gain permission from the school and also be able to explain what they are doing, what they are hoping to achieve and why.

LIBRARY BOOKS

One good use for some of the funds raised by the youth group could be to present some Christian books to the school library. These books could be any of the many good Christian books that your young people have found helpful and that they think their friends may read and find helpful too.

COMMUNITY ACTION

The Acts of the Apostles says of the early followers of Jesus that 'all the people spoke well of them'. Sadly this is often not the case with our churches today. The life of the church does not very often have much impact on people locally and, if this is true of the church, what about the youth group?

Active and positive community involvement is one way of counteracting this lack of community impact and of heightening people's awareness of what we stand for and what we do.

COMMUNITY YOUTH NOTICE BOARD

Church buildings have great potential because they are often centrally placed in the community. A youth notice board at the church could provide not only information about what is happening for the youth of the church but also be a focal point for youth activities generally in the area.

Details of all events of interest to the youth in the community could be placed on the board, e.g. concerts, raves, environmental projects, trips, youth clubs, what is on at the cinema or theatre, football teams – the potential is as endless as your community is varied. You may find that as soon as the board is up and working the list of things needing to be shown increases dramatically!

The noticeboard itself should be regularly updated and monitored but not necessarily censored. Word of mouth will soon get the information around the area that the board is the place to look to find out what is happening.

The advantages to the youth group of this are multiple: their own events can also be publicized on the board; other young people may see that church youngsters go to Lazerquest too; and young people find out where the board is and get used to where the church is and being seen in the vicinity of the church. The board itself can begin to be a means by which young people's views of church can be gently altered.

LITTER PICK AND TRASH BASH

Comunities often have areas of open space that are unsightly because of accumulated litter. These areas can provide an opportunity for you to do something for the community. Instead of arranging sponsorship for the task, why not just arrange for the youth group to have a Trash Bash? This will raise their own profile in the community and also improve the en-vironment for everyone. Your young people will probably have never noticed the mess before, in fact they probably couldn't really care less about it, but it is surprising how their attitudes will change after they have spent some of their free time clearing up the mess only to see someone else drop rubbish there!

You will, of course, need permission from the owners of the land (assuming it isn't church ground!) and you should also check your youth group insurance to see that you are covered for all eventualities.

You will need different coloured bags for different sorts of rubbish: e.g. cans, glass and metal can all be recycled. You will need to organize the transport to have all the rubbish taken to the appropriate recycling centre and to have any larger unrecyclables taken to the tip.

As with other events, you might use the local media to advertise what you have done. You may need to repeat the activity to ensure that the land remains in a cleared state. If the landowner is willing, why not see if your group can take responsibility for its upkeep? This sounds like a lot of work but it is a great team-building activity (moaning together about a task helps group cohesion!) and if you are the ones keeping the land tidy you may be able to use it for your own functions in the future, such as barbecues, bonfire parties, etc.

RETIREMENT HOME LINK

Older people have a lot to teach our young people (not that the youngsters will ever admit it), but all too often it is difficult to get the two groups together. A link with a retirement home can be useful for both parties. It should not simply involve the young people doing things for the older people; rather, it should be cultivated into a two-way relationship of learning, caring and discovery.

A good starter for building up the relationship is the good, old-fashioned Christmas singalong. Usually those in charge of running a retirement home are very willing to have groups of young people in to sing carols, read poems, do short pieces of drama and share readings at Christmas. This can even be the beginning of a tradition! If things go well and both groups hit it off, arrange for some of the keener members of your group to go round for part of an evening just to chat and play board games so that relationships can develop. These times should be kept fairly short at first, just to see how things go.

Further activities could include:

Reading

The young people could regularly read stories and articles to those whose eyesight has deteriorated. Reading to and talking with the older people can open young people's minds to views and experiences that are different from the ones they usually encounter.

Entertainment evening

The youth group could provide an evening of entertainment at the home itself: use songs, jokes, sketches, a singalong; and almost every youth group seems to own a juggler these days (among other specialized skills). Fit the entertainment to the special skills which your kids possess. Careful preparation and consideration are essential here, as is consultation with the staff at the retirement home as they will have useful ideas to help you on what will be enjoyed and what may or may not be appropriate.

Christmas party

This could provide an opportunity for an outing for the residents to your church premises. You need careful liaison with the staff at the home about the transport arrangements and any special care which those taking part may need.

Your group could combine with church members to provide

food, entertainment and carol singing. Decorate the room to festive standards and prepare to get together and have a good afternoon in each other's company.

Worship services

Occasional simple and short worship services can, if they are wanted, be another positive activity for both sides. This also has the benefit of encouraging your young people to consider themselves as service organizers, worship leaders and perhaps to have a go at giving a short talk, reading and sharing testimonies, etc.

Outings

Everyone loves an outing. When the weather is warm and the days are long, you could help your kids to organize a coach trip to the seaside or an evening trip to the theatre. Again, careful preparation, liaison and planning are required. If the youth group are to fund the trip itself, how will the money be raised? How long can the residents of the home comfortably travel for? Where would they like to go, if anywhere?

Birthday cards

Birthdays can be a lonely time for the elderly; gather a list of all those at the home you have contact with and ensure that they receive a birthday card from the youth group. If they do not have family and would otherwise be alone, why not see if a short visit would be possible?

NB Make sure your list of birthdays is kept up to date so that you know for sure that the prospective recipient of your birthday wishes is still at the home – this can avoid any embarrassing situations.

Developing this kind of relationship with a retirement home is not an easy option. It demands a lot of hard work and a certain level of commitment from your youth group. Choose activities suited to the commitment that your group would realistically feel able to give. Often carol singing at Christmas is as far as many groups feel they can go. If that is where your lot are, fine!

POLITICAL ACTION

The Gospel is highly political. Jesus often challenged both the religious and political assumptions of those around him. Ignoring an issue can be just as much a political statement as supporting or opposing it. As Edmund Burke once said: 'For the triumph of evil it is only necessary that good men do nothing'.

By 'political action' I do not mean party-political, but action that challenges, questions or opposes all society's values and activities that are in contradiction to God's values.

ARRESTING FAST

As an act of solidarity with the many Christians overseas in captivity for their faith, and also to raise awareness of their situation, why not hold a twenty-four-hour fast with a difference?

Ask your local community policeman to help you to arrange for some of the group to spend twenty-four hours in a police cell with only water to sustain them for the time. The remainder of the group can be involved by setting up a vigil nearby: talking to passers-by, raising funds, and singing freedom-type songs (there is a wealth of material in the Wild Goose Songbooks, produced by the Iona Community).

Contact your mission organizations linked to your church or Amnesty International for details of individual cases that you can focus on and to whom you can send the money you raise.

You never know, the event could have such an impact on your group, congregation, police or community that the cause could be taken to heart for longer than the event itself!

NOT JUST THEATRE

Street theatre is a great way to have fun and raise people's awareness at the same time. If you have young people with dramatic or musical talent or circus skills, get them together to brainstorm some ideas. Look at issues they are concerned about and convert these into sketches. This sounds a daunting task at first but you will often be surprised at how inventive and resourceful your young people can be, and also what excellent material they can come up with! Do not be disheartened if it takes them a little while to get going or to get the hang of transferring their ideas into drama . . . stick with it and it will all slot into place eventually.

After you have your sketches, rehearse so that the young people are confident enough to get out onto the street.

Street theatre needs to be highly visual, simple, attention-grabbing and challenging. There are many issues that are suitable for basing your theatre on: homelessness, poverty, Third World debt, the destruction of the rainforest and ozone layer, and other environmental issues. The list is endless.

This kind of theatre has a 'hit and run' feel to it. Make sure your drama is short and full of impact, challenging those who see it to think about the issues you are portraying. This can be another excellent awareness raiser, but it needs to be done well to have a good effect. When it all goes well, your young people will swell in confidence and probably want to do a lot more of it. It's quite addictive!

LETTER WRITING

Those who are in political power in councils or in government are often extremely sensitive to public opinion. Letter writing is one way we can demonstrate the strength of our feelings on an issue. The issues your young people write about will depend on the concerns they have. They may be community concerns, e.g. lack of facilities for young people, homelessness, environmental issues; or it might be that a crucial vote is coming up in the House of Commons – often on issues like abortion. MPs have a free vote and may be swayed by letters they receive.

JOIN A POLITICAL PARTY

All the political parties have youth movements attached to them. One way to further Kingdom values and to influence decisions is to get involved with any of these. Issues are discussed and motions can be raised at National Youth Conferences.

MP'S SURGERY

This is not a chance to chop off your MP's tongue and divide it into small pieces, but an opportunity for young people to talk to their Member of Parliament in person. Many MPs of all parties will be willing to come to your youth group to face questions and talk about issues, but they will obviously need plenty of notice.

This is a great opportunity for the young people to raise a number of issues and concerns and really feel that they are getting somewhere. If your MP is unable to visit you, then visit him or her with a delegation from your youth group next time your MP has a 'surgery'. Most MPs hold these fairly regularly, often on Saturdays.

As well as your team of questioners, perhaps try videoing the discussion (although you will need to get advance permission to do this) to show to the rest of the youth group or church later.

ABORTION

There are a number of Christian organizations that are active in the field of care and support for single mothers as well as in campaigning for the sanctity of unborn life. Many have videos and discussion material available to youth groups as well as gifted and educated speakers who will visit your group to look at this issue.

This is one area in which the views of the world are very much at odds with those of Christians. Young people need support and education to know why life is sacred and how to defend their beliefs and values, as they can often feel defeated and think that there is nothing they can do to turn the tide in this area.

For more information you can contact:

Care Trust
53 Romney Street
London
SW1P 3RF

Life
Life House
Newbold Terrace
Leamington Spa
Warwickshire
CV32 4EA

PRAYER ACTION

Prayer is a vital part of the Christian life. It does not always have to be just 'Heads down, hands together, eyes shut, now shush'. Jesus' prayers were often dynamic and active, at other times quiet and contemplative. It is a good exercise for young people to look at how Jesus prayed and to think about modelling their own prayers on some of his.

PRAYER PHOTOS

Before the group next meets, send two young people out into your town or village armed with an instant camera to photograph buildings, places and people that they feel it is important to pray for. They might want to photograph an old people's home, the police force, a local amusement arcade, a place where homeless people sleep: the choice is theirs.

On the evening when your group meets, place the photographs round the room with a number next to each one. Give each member a pencil and paper on which to write what each of the places or buildings are or who the people are, and why they think it is important that they are prayed for.

Divide into groups of three or four people and give each group some of the numbers to pray for. After a time of prayer (the length and style of which will depend upon your group), encourage the young people to take their lists home and use them in their daily prayers.

This method can also be used as a mechanism for the group to pray for their non-Christian friends, their families, church members or each other. Take photos of these people, number the photos and put all the numbers into a hat. Each group member then draws a number and agrees to pray for that person once a day for a week.

CANDLE PRAYERS

Candles have been used as symbols in worship since the earliest days of Christianity and simple prayers around a candle can be a very effective way of encouraging your young people both to pray and also not to feel self-conscious about praying, as the room will be semi-dark!

If your group has 25 members or fewer, sit around a single candle. If your group is larger than this, perhaps you will need to have more than one candle and to divide into groups.

Ask the young people to sit and pass out pens and paper. Ask them to write down one area of darkness in the world and then place that piece of paper on the floor round the candle. Ask members to read out the pieces of paper and then those who wish to can pray for some of the areas that have been named.

End with the Lord's Prayer, or a chorus or song that everyone knows.

PLACE AND TIME PRAYERS

A long time before it was light, Jesus got up to pray (Mark 1:35)

Young people are not usually morning people, but early morning can be a great time to pray. Hold a dawn prayer meeting on top of a local hill, mountain, tall building, or in a park – anywhere out in the open. Perhaps arrange to get up before dawn, walk there, have your prayer meeting and then go somewhere for breakfast afterwards. Food is always a good incentive!

Pray for what you can see from your venue and for what you saw on the way. You could also use short 'thank you' prayers for all the good things that happen.

Depending on your area and also on the age of your young people, hold a night-time prayer meeting at about 2.00 am in church. Arrange soft lights and perhaps candles. Pray for those who are in darkness, for those who have to work at night and for those beginning the day in other parts of the world. It might be a good idea to notify the local police and any other church neighbours that you will be doing this, as well as your minister, deacons, church wardens etc. Perhaps your minister or congregation members would like to come along.

PRAYER CALENDAR

Ask each of your group members to list anonymously their top three prayer concerns. Collate these and produce a prayer calendar for the month with a different person, issue or thing to pray for each day. You will need perhaps to be flexible with some of the suggestions and make them appropriate for the group.

GROUP ACTION

CHILD SPONSORSHIP

The youth group might like to pledge an amount of money each month to support an individual child in the Third World rather than support a project. This money ensures that the child will be fed, clothed, housed and educated as well as exposed to the Gospel.

The advantages can be many. It is easy to raise the relatively small sums necessary to fund such sponsorship, and even if the personalities in your group change, the project can still have continuity. The link is with a specific individual and hence the benefits are more easily apparent. It is often possible to write to the child and send Christmas or birthday presents, and to receive letters in return. In addition your group will receive updates on the sponsorship from the organization concerned. Child sponsorship is a very youth group-friendly way of showing concern for the Third World.

However, as with all things, sponsorship can have its disadvantages. There are those who would rather support a project as opposed to an individual, as they do not want to single one person out for special treatment. There are many opportunities through organizations such as Tearfund, Christian Aid and Interserve to give a small but regular amount to a project or for a specific purpose.

JUBILEE FUND

This is based on the biblical notion of jubilee (Leviticus 25:11–55). A Jubilee Fund is an amount of money which is set aside to help those in need. This could be used for subsidizing members of your group to participate in residential events that they would not otherwise be able to afford. It could also be for others beyond the reach of the group but who are known to be in need, or for special needs or emergencies, e.g. a local child who needs an operation or a disaster overseas.

The income to the fund will need to be fairly constant. This could come as a percentage tithe from subs or tuck-shop profits, or perhaps from income from special events like Miss-A-Meal. Your group members could decide how the fund should operate and to whom the money should go.

As the fund is administered, questions will be raised like: 'What are God's priorities?' and 'What kind of issues or people would Jesus be concerned about?' Through these and other sticky questions, our groups begin to ground their faith in real-life issues and situations that they have to make practical decisions about.

COMPUTER GAME EXCHANGE

Young people in youth groups often exchange or lend each other tapes, CDs, videos and computer disks and games. Why not tax these exchanges and make this natural process a beneficial one for the whole group or for a Jubilee Fund or Third World project?

Items people are willing to lend or exchange are listed on a notice board and whenever an item is exchanged, an amount is placed in the 'tax box'.

The object of the exercise is threefold:

* To raise awareness that there are luxuries which most of the world does without.
* To raise funds for a good cause.
* To point out to the youth group that illegal copying is as much a breach of Deuteronomy 5:19 as pinching sweets from the local shop or holding up a bank!

LOVE CHURCH WEEK

Youth groups are often rightly frustrated with their churches, whether because of the slowness of the decision-making process, a failure to be dynamic or just the worship style. However, sometimes their frustration can be more from rebellion than righteousness.

God loves his Church and the youth group is part of that Church. Why not change the habit of a lifetime and have a Love Church Week? This is best done at some point during the school holidays when the young people have a little more time on their hands.

Love Church can include:

* Some young people going to all of the services; yes, even the *really* boring ones in the middle of the week and aiming to talk with some of the congregations afterwards.
* The young people not sitting together as a clique but spreading out throughout the congregation.
* Visiting people on the visiting list.

- Cleaning and tidying youth group cupboards.
- Joining the church and hall cleaning team for a week.
- Taking the minister and his family out for pizza.
- Attending a prayer meeting.
- Tidying the church garden.
- Serving coffee and cakes free (!) after the Sunday service to say thank you for all the church does.

ENVIRONMENTAL ACTION

One of the characteristics of today's society is that 'issues' and politics have joined music and clothes as victims of what is 'in fashion'. What is *in* one week is *out* the next. Unfortunately, the media can make anything news for just a week, and so almost everything becomes trivialized and devalued. Environmental issues have not escaped this: what was last week's news is now out of the limelight.

As Christians, who should be committed to being stewards of God's earth, we cannot pass by on the other side just because the action is no longer in vogue. This is especially true if passing by denies important truths about the nature of God. Our neglect of the environmental issue leaves the field open to the New Age prophets and the anti-Christian gurus, and shows the world that God has no concern for his world.

The problems we have as youth leaders are often made more difficult by the experiences of our young people. I asked the Senior Christian Union at school about what issues or topics they might wish to be included in the term's programme: the reply came back unanimously, 'Nothing Green – we're sick to death of it at school!' They had been force-fed environmental issues at school and by the media until they had not only been bored by it but also desensitized to it. Others, however, are keen to get radical in this area. It is important that we, as youth leaders, know where each of our young people stand between these two extremes and choose our activities to suit.

This still leaves us with the question: 'How can we, as youth leaders, do anything radical and environmental if our young people are totally bored with the issues or have already done all the exciting and fun things we can think of?'

1. Our programmes should not be primarily about entertaining our youngsters but about discipling them. There are plenty of worthwhile things we can do that are unpleasant, grubby and at first unattractive but that demonstrate our concern as stewards of God's earth. These are also things we can have great fun doing, not because fun is the objective but it is a by-product of being and doing things together.

2. We need to see concerns for our world in a different context from school or the media. Our approach must challenge and change lives and lifestyles. Recycling cans is good, but should we be using disposable packaging (it uses almost as much energy to recycle them)? Are the contents of the packaging fairly traded? What price was paid to the people who produced the ingredients and what was the environmental impact on the countries that produced them? What about *my life*, and *my life-style* when the kids come round for Bible study? Does what I say and what I do about the environmental issues add up? We can't expect our young people to get excited and angry about issues if we ourselves don't care.

3. Action cannot be imposed on our members. We may think that something is a great idea but unless the whole group can identify with your idea as worthwhile and participate in the planning and preparation before doing the project, it will fail even before it starts. Merely getting the task done is not what it is all about. The processes involved are equally if not more important. It is in the process that the young people do theology as they ask: 'Why is God concerned?' 'Where in the Bible does it say . . . why can't we . . . what about . . . should we try?'

The activities suggested in this section are by no means exhaustive or original but they are ways in which various church youth groups have tried to be active stewards of creation.

INTRODUCE YOUR GROUP TO THE ISSUES

Write out the following suggestions onto A4 sheets of paper and put them up round the room for your group to consider. Are these something we would like to get involved in? What are the pros and cons of such actions? Do we think any of these are worthwhile? Use them as a discussion starter.

The following ideas have been coded:

I – indicates specifically an individual action

G – indicates specifically a group action

C – indicates specifically a community action

F – indicates specifically a faith-orientated action.

Eat less meat (I)

It takes 10 kg of vegetable protein to produce 1 kg of animal protein. Therefore, the less meat we eat, the more food will be available for others.

Use recycled paper (G)

Recycle paper as a group or perhaps set a target for a quantity of paper to be recycled in a given time. Six tons of paper recycled saves one hundred trees – try to recycle that much in six weeks. Why not challenge another youth group to see who can save the most trees by recycling the most paper?

The more the demand for recycled paper products, the greater will be the effort from the business world to encourage recycling and fewer trees will consequently need to be felled for paper.

Plant a tree (G)

We worry about the rainforests being destroyed. The forests here in Britain have already been destroyed; why not help reverse the trend by planting a tree.

Save water (I/family)

Placing a large pebble in your toilet cistern will save that amount of water each flush. Multiply that by the approximate number of flushes per year to calculate the amount of water saved.

Use the shower (I)

Use the shower instead of the bath: it saves water.

Be animal friendly (I/G)

Buy only products that have not been tested on animals and avoid stores that are not concerned about it. Check also that the ingredients of products bought have not been tested on animals, as some companies advertise their products as being 'animal friendly' but manufacture the product using ingredients that aren't.

Volunteer (G/I)

Volunteer to spend the day with conservation volunteers, the Woodland Trust or National Park helpers working on the environment.

Batteries are included (I)

Use only rechargeable batteries for your Walkman, torch etc. These work out cheaper in the long term and do not produce the harmful heavy metals produced by the throw-away batteries.

Can collection (C)

Collect aluminium cans for recycling: pay a small amount to members and non-members who collect them to encourage collection.

Say no (G/I)

Say no to overpackaged goods.

Organize a worship service (F)

Ask if you can run a service on environmental issues, demonstrating God's concern for his creation.

Say no (I)

Say no to apathy.

Say no (I/G)

Say no to giving up when it ceases to be trendy to be concerned for God's world and the media have moved on to the latest entertainment news.

Pray for forgiveness (F/I)

Pray for forgiveness for your part in the failure to be a proper steward of God's creation.

Get angry (I)

God has given us our emotions; it is OK to be angry at what is happening in his world. We can weep in prayer over the devastation of rainforests and scream at the injustices that let our brother and sisters in Christ die from starvation when there is enough food available to feed everyone.

Walk to church (I)

Instead of getting a lift, walk or cycle to church. It is good for you and good for the world.

Church car share scheme (G)

The youth group provides the administration for this project. The idea is that several people travel together to or from work in the same car.

1. Use church notice boards, the church magazine, drama or the notices slot during services to provide information on the savings and advantages to the world of reduced car usage.

2. Carry out a survey of where people work, when and how they travel and if they would be interested in the possibility of car sharing.

3. Work out what is theoretically possible and practical in

terms of shared car journeys and talk with the people concerned to see how they feel about the suggested arrangements.

4. When all is agreed, pin up the details on the notice board. Add a running weekly or monthly total of either car miles or journeys that have been saved. Even with only a few participants, the number of car journeys saved over a year can be huge.

5. See if any of those participants who are saving money would like to contribute their savings (or some of their savings) to the youth group, Jubilee Fund or charity.

6. Make sure that there is provision for new people to join the scheme wherever possible and also for existing participants to pull out if they want to. Or perhaps run the scheme for an initial trial period and see how it goes. You never know, maybe the people involved will want to make it a regular habit!

Eco-activists

Form a group of young people as a sort of 'working party' to monitor environmental issues and information (either local ones or something of a wider nature) and to report back to the youth group with ideas for action. This might be writing letters, campaigning, replanting, cleaning up, praying or demonstrating.

This has the advantage that the concerns adopted will be of concern to the young people and they are therefore more likely to adopt them wholeheartedly.